Time for God

"Effective Steps to a Productive Life"

Joe Luna

visit - www.timeforgodbook.com

Dedication

- This book is dedicated to Jesus Christ
- To my wife Angela for her loving support and warm spirit
- And especially my two sons Noah and Elijah, for being so incredible

Table of Contents

Chapter 1 – Organization 1

Chapter 2 – Clarity 17

Chapter 3 – Direction..27

Chapter 4 – Prioritized Action......................................40

Chapter 5 – Reduction 61

Chapter 6 – Conflicts...75

Chapter 7 – Completion..85

Chapter 8 – Focus...95

Chapter 9 – Transformation 102

Notes 119

Index..129

Credits & Thanks..133

Scripture References...135

Do You Believe In Jesus?..139

Chapter 1 – Organization

"Order my steps in thy word: and let not any iniquity have dominion over me."
Psalm 119:133 KJV

In our life right now, we've experienced a rapid transition from the age of information to the age of attention. There's been a worldwide shift and as experts study the effects … it's hugely significant to followers of Christ like you and I. Today, we encounter more new information daily than a highly-educated person would have their whole life in the 18th century. To make it worse, the information pushed on us isn't by request. It's a strategic plan to take captive the thoughts, actions, and directions of our lives.

What's even more disturbing is that the competition for our attention is getting fiercer by the minute. It starts in advertising, sneaks into our families, then streams out everywhere else we look. We need a plan to focus our eyes on what matters as the pulse of the world speeds up.

Today, our attention is directed *for us* and we have way too much information available *to us*. Information is almost worthless now. It's been devalued because it's everywhere. At one point, when information was hard to get, people would give a lot to get it. The value it once had is lost because we can get information quicker and easier today.

It's helpful to have what we need quickly, but we also have what we don't need right in front of us … and the world is begging us to choose the latter. That's the drawback. The increase in unusable information is almost overwhelming. This same pattern is increasing in people's lives. Information whenever we want it can bring us to a point where we almost stop making progress. Information actually tricks us into thinking we're productive and that we,*" know what's going on"*, but when our attention is going the wrong way and there is too much information, it just leads to complication.

For instance, we know from the history books that when the Greek statesman Demosthenes spoke to the masses, people said, *"What a fine speaker he is"* and he impacted the lives of many. But not too many people's lives are impacted by Demosthenes today. He forgot God. The most important choice he made in life was tragic.

That's an example of too much attention on the wrong information. It's complication and that leads to a life misdirected. What was true for the Greeks is also true for society today. On the other hand, when Jesus Christ spoke … he gave eternal *wisdom*. That *wisdom* is still present in the lives of millions of his followers to this very day.

By picking up this book, you're signaling that you are a leader, ready to take action, and you realize this problem. Whether you see the factors in your career, ministry, or personal life, you've noticed all of the outside influences prying their way into your life. It's time to strip down to what brings eternal value for you and those you care about.

With that said, you have a choice to make right now:

1. You can stay on the same path you've been going down
2. … or you can take the opportunity to get the value from this book and apply it to your life

This book leads to something better and ultimately to the timeless truth of Jesus Christ

We may be living in this age of attention but Jesus Christ placed us here specifically for something more … <u>*transformation.*</u> In order for that transformation to take place, we have to focus our attention in the right direction … as the proverb goes:

"for the Lord gives wisdom, and from his mouth come knowledge and understanding."

In the modern jungle of information and attention deficits, without eternal wisdom, a person can make bad choices, invest poorly, and misuse resources. It's critical for us to have the focused words of the Bible present in our lives. It allows for us to be confident, measured, and tactical in our daily walk with Christ.

Read Romans 6:23. It's time to get real. Life ultimately leads to two destinations: Heaven or Hell. There is no in-between. This battle for your attention is a strategic one that can steal real souls of living people you and I love. If one is distracted long enough they may miss that single critical point of wisdom. Each day that we've been given is something unique that we can't reclaim once it's gone. We're commanded to make the most of each one.

The Goal

As you go through the entire process, do each exercise, and put to work the biblical principles and methods I'm going to show you … you will become twice as productive as you are right now, even if you already have a good amount of direction in your family, your work-life, and your contribution to Christ. This process will help you challenge the reasons why you do the things you do and provide methods to help provoke behavior change, one step at a time.

So let me say that again. The goal of this program is: To engage with it, take the methods I'm going to teach you, complete the exercises and use what you learn - then, to become twice as effective as you already are. Getting much more done with more focus time and better output, even with all of the modern distractions, cultural influences, and all of the "world" going on around you. _And it will all be to serve the singular purpose of who you are as a disciple of Jesus Christ._

Because every one of us has come to a point in our lives when we've hit a ceiling. When the complexities of life or the lack of direction coincide with the inability to move forward in those things that matter most to us.

- Doing more doesn't help
- Working faster makes things worse

- Pushing harder doesn't do it either

We need to find the way out.

The good news is we have answers as followers of Christ. You have an unfair advantage when it comes to managing life and getting ahead. *You know the author!* But the answer doesn't come without the proper questions and a few of them can be gained from Matthew 8:18-22. Read it then ask yourself the following questions …

- Are you willing to obey the timeless wisdom of Jesus Christ?
- Are you ready to make significant changes?
- Are you able to persevere even when it gets tough?

If you are willing to do all three of these things … let's get started.

God is a God of Order

The Bible begins with God's progressive order and balance in creating the world and mankind. From there, organization is a clear characteristic of who God is. Look at the Ten Commandments … the covenants established with Abraham and throughout the Bible … how about the pattern of prayer in Matthew 6:5 … the Tabernacle's order and Hebrews 8:5 … some historians note that without God as a God of order, science wouldn't exist … the list goes on.

As a Christian, you need to uncover the wisdom to work smarter, to simplify, and to focus your life only on what will be most productive. You will learn how to advance yourself in the right direction, setting you on a higher plateau to get more accomplished in what you intend to achieve. You'll do this by patterning your life in God's will.

… you're going to have to leave some things behind.

You will have to redefine what you value as "better", and it will take effort. I promise you that. You're going to have to boldly step out of yourself and into the model of Jesus Christ and the wisdom he's left us in order to live a biblically successful life. To do that you're going to purposefully direct yourself to regain your God-given freedom.

You will have some personal transformations that occur in the process. Once you learn these, you will be able to take them and re-use them at a later date to reorganize and regain your freedom as the world tries to clutter you up.

A Simple Concept

So, let's get started with how you can get the most out of this process by understanding a simple method.

There's one key concept you need to internalize. If you're going to become more successful in your life as a Christian, more productive and effective, then you need to understand one simple point. The distinction is the difference between *studying on*, *studying in*, and *studying out*.

Each day as you're learning there will be a time when we're going to be *studying on* or … reading … absorbing … taking in the material.

Then there will be a time where you are going to be *studying in* or … doing the exercises … meditating on and challenging your heart and mind … bouncing the ideas around … comprehending and internalizing the scripture and material. This is where you can allow your current beliefs and thoughts to be shaped by the scriptural truths and the ideas of this book.

Then the most important part for you is, when you *study out* or … take action … apply the truth … implement it in your life. This is where internal change causes and external transformation to occur.

If you're not taking this process and *studying on, in, and out,* then one of us can be doing something better! Let's start by doing our best together. I want to make this learning idea clear. Make sure you take what you learn and go into your life and use it!

These three ideas of *studying on, in, and out* work together. For example: *Studying on* and hearing Matthew 6:6 leads to *studying in* and the desire to meditate on scripture which in turn relates to *studying out* and the disciplined practice of praying in private. Keep in mind these disciplines don't always come overnight. They do come in time as long as you seat the truths in your heart.

Start thinking from these three perspectives now …

So, you can understand the different views in relationship to each other and you need all three perspectives to make the most progress. Make sure you're doing your best to shift your perspective throughout the program. Looking at things from three views may sound like a lot, but 1 Corinthians 2:16 says:

"...But we have the mind of Christ."

I believe that together we can make it happen.

The Challenge

There's a personal issue we have today. An increasing problem I've noticed with the world and my own life at times is that there's a decrease in the ability to connect the dots. Here's what I mean: There are three core sources for how we connect our dots in life: Godly **wisdom**, man's **knowledge**, and our **information** driven culture. Sometimes, the only thing that makes it in front of us is the immediacy of our information driven culture.

A man once said," I look at the Bible and the news so I can see what both sides are up to ..."

At the same time, God's wisdom can be plainly available, but usually it is veiled by the clutter of information. The worst part is that culture and wisdom (in almost all cases) are like black and white. If you use up all your time focused on cultural information, you will end up falling behind and disappointed. You're challenge is to reconnect the dots and it may not be easy. It may be counter-intuitive to what you want to do. But, if you're going to approach life correctly, you must come from this position.

Look to what Jesus says in Matthew 17:20. Using faith right moves mountains, but sometimes we're too busy focusing our light on anthills with a magnifying glass.

Even Archimedes, the philosopher, got it right when he said:

"Give me a lever long enough and a fulcrum on which to place it, and I shall move the world."

Your leverage is your faith and your foundation is Jesus. You're going to focus your energy on getting more meaningful activity out of the same amount of time so you can experience God moving those mountains. Like the Bible, if you take the practical advice from this book into your daily life, you'll see the results.

Here's something I've had in common with others. There was a time in my life when I actually thought freedom meant not having to do anything. Have you ever had that feeling? I really thought that at one point I would feel so successful or independently free that I would be happy doing nothing! Well, as it turns out that's not true. Studies on retirement show that when people retire they usually do nothing, they get bored, and then become boring.

In the Army, if you serve 20 years you can retire pretty young. Sadly enough, I've read studies of retirees dying prematurely because they go stagnant from their formerly active military lifestyle. The people I know that are the happiest are actually the most effective and free.

Renewal and relaxation is important, but not focus #1. I want you to become the best you've ever been, and also the most effective you've ever been. Think of an athlete that's impacting the team by being the best on the field. Or an actor who makes a film and changes the hearts and minds of millions with just one role. Think Jesus' three-year ministry that changed your life!

Psalms 5:12 gives us the guidance. As we begin, I'd like for you to go ahead and *take note of this psalm*. This is going to be your shield. One possible barrier to productivity is completing our righteous efforts (we'll go into detail on that later). For now, I ask that you place this prayer somewhere prominent as you get started. Make sure you have your Bible available each day as we explore the scriptures and ideas together.

Exercises

So let's move on to your game plan and some basic clean up. Go through the 5 points below and if there are areas that are causing frustration, challenges, or disorganization in your life, let's start by clearing those up first.

1. **You will see the best results if you keep things fairly simple.** Fight the spirit of "overwhelm" and of "complication". As you go through the process, if you just master a fraction of what is contained within the pages of this book, you will markedly enhance your productivity. Keep that top of mind. *What areas of your life can you cut the overwhelm and complication right now?*

2. **Do you need more or less?** The world knows how to push our buttons and keep us on it's pace. The reality is that almost everything can wait. Understand that the important decisions in life stand out and you don't need to pay attention to every sense of urgency that's around you, so look for sources of manufactured urgency and start recognizing them now. Have you been caught in a pattern of waiting for the world to tell you what to do? Or are you too busy taking care of everything that's on your plate? _What areas of your life can you quickly slow down or speed up in order to be more productive?_

3. **Start to finish.** Most people today don't finish books they buy, that's the difference between you and them. You're going to succeed in this undertaking by moving forward one step at a time and understanding that the "next big thing" that may catch everyone else's eye isn't going to be better for you, it's just going to hinder you from moving forward. Most people get caught in cycles of taking on too many projects and never finishing one. You're going to get to the finish by finding that out now! _What plan will you set to make sure you finish this book?_

4. **Get rid of junk**. Whether it's your office, computer, refrigerator, closet or car, get organized and trim the fat from your life now. From this one simple step you will get ahead before we even begin. Get rid of the useless stuff that has accumulated. If you can't quickly tell yourself that it's providing value to you or someone else in your life in a good way, it's got to go! _How much junk can you get rid of today?_

5. **Make sense of everything!** If you have writing pads ... well, only use one pad and put it next to the pencils. If you spend too much time making dinner, find something else to cook! Begin to rethink how you approach life right now as you advance into the wisdom and methods we'll explore. Your goal is clarity, freedom and a shift away from busyness, waste and the abuses that so often go unnoticed. *How much more clarity can you bring to your life just by rethinking things?*

Don't forget to convince yourself you can do it! Belief is the most powerful and influential weapon that God has given us to overcome any battle that we are going to win. As you move forward in this journey, go into it with the expectation that it's already done. Jesus told us to pray like our prayers have been answered and our belief in righteous undertakings should be the same way.

Next

We're going to use a simple three step technique throughout this book (just remember the three P's). We'll use it in different ways. You may recognize it or you may not as you're going through. It's going to challenge us to get the most out of each day and be the best disciples we can be. It's very simple and very effective.

1. Plan
2. Prioritize (when we prioritize ... we can get specific below)
    a. Define the purpose
    b. Find the needs
    c. Identify the problems

    d. Gather resources

    e. Build habits

    f.   Establish a budget/limits

    g. Set a timeline

    h. Take action

3. Purge

This is the process God used when he chose Noah to build the ark, brought forth the animals of every kind, and flooded the earth. It's a biblical pattern you can pick up on if you look closely enough throughout the Bible. Read Genesis 6, 7 & 8. Review the 3 step plan above and match the verses to the steps. It's the same process we saw God gave Moses in the constructing of the Tabernacle to purge sin. The process itself relates to all of us when things begin to get disorganized and chaotic in life. Use it! You might not always need all of the (a-h) sub-points under the Prioritize step but this is where you begin to pattern after the order of God.

From here, let's begin by getting rid of the biggest thing that is drawing from your relationship with God:

    1. What area of your life consumes too much of your time and takes your focus off of God?

Next, let's ask some more questions to help uncover why that's important to minimize or completely eliminate:

    2. What problems or issues does this cause for you now?

3. What will you gain if you wasted less time focused on that area?

4. What do you see when you imagine yourself even more focused in the will of God and the satisfaction it will bring?

Next, it's time to take action by organizing how you will reduce your time spent in this area. You will do this by starting with all the little things that come to your mind right now that you can knock-out with one punch. Don't mull over this. Then you won't get anything done. Just start doing it right now.

If your focus area is a *specific relationship*, you might start with forgiving someone … repenting to God … setting time to read about relationships or healing in the Bible …

If your focus area is *time management*, you might start with setting time limits … using idle time for a purpose like reading or catching up on calls … planning your days a day ahead … make a to-do list so you don't have to rely on your memory … doing similar activities at the same time … creating a reward structure for progress you make …

If your focus area is *your home*, you might start with cleaning file cabinet, drawers, or records … gathering all of your books on Christianity … rearranging your desk … consolidating calendars … using a desk organizer …

If your focus area is *anxiety,* you might start with telling someone "no" to additional commitments ... calling the people who send you junk to get off of their lists ... scheduling uninterrupted focus time ... handing-off unimportant tasks ... setting a time to relax . . .

... set up the initial conditions that will lead to your success.

Let me close here and tell you about how to get the most from this program. The book is broken down into a series of chapters that was designed to be progressive. If you are having trouble in a specific area you may feel like you want to hop to that chapter. I would recommend that you will get the biggest reward if you read this book from front to back. You can complete it as quickly as you can effectively consume it. Start now.

Key objectives from this chapter
Received a brief introduction
Understood the biblical basis for organization
Determined your focus area

Chapter 2 – Clarity

"But as for you, the Lord took you and brought you out of the iron-smelting furnace, out of Egypt, to be the people of his inheritance, as you now are."

Deuteronomy 4:20

When buying a diamond, clarity is a critical factor. It may be the difference between a *"WOW"* and an *"Oh, that's nice."*. If someone doesn't look too close, sometimes a lack of clarity can slide by unnoticed. The small defects can't really be seen. As you get closer and focus in, you begin to see more and that's where clarity counts.

A lack of clarity in life is like being in bondage. Your freedom isn't really free because you don't know where you're headed. The Israelites were in bondage to the Egyptians … they were slaves held captive in their actions by a ruthless oppressor. Then, Moses led them out of bondage and into the desert, but they were still captives . . . to their minds. They were busy looking backwards and they lacked belief. Read Hebrews 3:16, 18-19.

Like the Israelites in the wilderness, we are between a promise and the fulfillment of that promise. Like them, we have been de-

livered from a ruthless oppressor, but we haven't reached our final destination. Are you wandering or are you walking in clarity?

A person can't enter the promised land without leaving Egypt.
The Israelites turned back when the road ahead looked difficult.
They failed to obey God's instructions and trust in his promise ...
they wandered, but they got there. There's a good possibility
you can gain more clarity and wander less. We all can to some
degree. Guess what? God had a plan for them *and he has one for
us*. Let's not wander.

When Jesus celebrated Passover, he transformed it. He displayed
what redemption, communion, and service really meant through
his time here on earth. You and I are continually in communion
with something. The situations we end up in are all branches of
our spiritual beliefs. The thoughts that really drive our body to
produce fruit in life. That's really where our clutter stems from.
We need a good "summer trimming". Each choice in life is a
choice toward freedom or toward bondage. There is no middle
realm; we're investing in one or the other at all times.

Are There Benefits to a Lack of Clarity?

It's pretty easy to measure the benefits of freedom and clarity. It
can be calculated in our daily lives in terms of finance, vitality or
even free time. Whether its getting a promotion or spending
time with your family, these choices deliver something tangible.

Unfortunately, bondage and a lack of clarity have no benefits.
We have to look backwards to the conditions that led us to there
to even measure something tangible in our lives. Then, it
becomes very vivid to us that they are negative: inaction, fear,

and confusion to name a few. Take a look at those three conditions and pause a moment to see if you can come up with any benefits that come out of them.

My guess is there aren't any.

The biggest issue we have is that these things slip by us unnoticed and they take a chunk of today with them. Not having clarity actually has a steep price of stealing your life and you pay with every fiber of your being.

Become a bond-servant to Christ and release yourself from bondage

We should only bind ourselves to Jesus. The apostle Paul in Romans 1:1 used one of the most slavish terms possible when describing this bond to Christ. This bond releases us from the conditions of bondage and into the mercy of God. Take fear as an example. Our culture has told us that it's okay to be afraid and that we should rely on the newspaper, television and word-of-mouth. We've actually learned to rely on the world and it's systems to such a point that it takes away from who we were meant to be in Christ.

That's because the spirit of fear is learned through bondage.

Just recently I noticed several back-to-back events that help build this pattern of fear in people's lives.

- Multiple speakers discussing panic, fear, and the structural collapse of world systems that people are reliant upon

- The Wall Street Journal talking about the "Fear epidemic"

- Dozens of magazine covers amplifying the "state of fear" in our nation

- Television media building on "fear" stories for ratings

Like race horses with blinders we've got to be focused on the finish line.

We've got to filter what we're taking in because everything we take in counts. When we allow fear to enter our lives, it creates a learned sense of reliance. It leads to a sense of helplessness in what we do and spreads the lie that we are helpless. Really what it's doing is allowing for the acceptance of excuses. Here's the truth: *"We can overcome any situation through Jesus Christ"*.

How to Clear the Fear . . .

Former Harvard psychologist Jerome Brunner was noted as saying, *"You're more likely to act yourself into a feeling than to feel yourself into action."*

What Dr. Brunner is trying to get across, is that when fear overwhelms, it causes inaction. On the other hand, sometimes we try to manufacture emotions to get ourselves going, but that only works sometimes. We have to realize that it's not the world, emotions, or anything other than our faith in Christ that should direct our movement.

The good news is that through Christ you're more resourceful than you can imagine. Read what the Bible tells us in Philippians

6:11. Jesus planned for you to use the armor of God to advance in what's truly important in your life. In order to overcome fear, inaction and confusion, we've got to bring it back to the basics and fight with the weapons God's given us. Think of the bold way little toddlers run at everything they do. That's how I want to be!

Fail for Jesus to overcome fear

Here's a revelation that hold's some of us back … God didn't guarantee we'd win all the battles … just the war. Even in failure we can be confident in our direction. Rather than sulking in fear or past failures or what you haven't even attempted yet, look back and step forward. It helps us to fail fast, learn, and do it again. It not only softens the emotions of failure, it also helps you feel good about overcoming obstacles as you see what went wrong and how you can do things better next time.

Sometimes failure is a result of not working hard enough. Often, failure is a way to get better. We're all meant to shine for Jesus but sometimes we lose sight of the fact that it can get really hard at times. The trick is to understand that failure is just a more intelligent way to begin again.

From there you can get strategic with failure. You can take failure to a point where it invigorates you for the next time you have the opportunity to fail. You can come at your fear from another angle. Think in unique ways … ask others for input … make a plan … make it fun!

Avoid Comfort

Sometimes people make a choice to be in bondage. This is a decision of comfort over freedom. The type of comfort I'm talking about is inaction. The problem with comfort is some have settled for it way to early. And it can give someone a feeling that they were born to be mediocre. *But you were made in the unique image of God.*

Just the other day I was at a retirement home visiting my mother-in-law. When I do that I try to visit the Alzheimer's Ward and I feel good knowing that Jesus even has a plan for those who have lost their memory. Visualizing how beautifully God has created us and his plan brings me to a question," *If I were to forget everything I knew about the past ... how old would I feel?"*

We are a culmination of our experiences. And if we wipe clean what was behind us, it's a re-birthing to look at the future with new eyes. It allows for a sense of invigorated freedom that we can do all things in Jesus Christ. Listen, Jesus isn't looking at your failures. If you see someone else doing something bigger in life, instead of looking up to them, look up to Jesus and ask him, *"What's stopping me".*

- There are people who are 62 that skydive, go to college, and evangelize ... they are young
- Some 23 year-old's defend bad ideals and are set in their ways ... they are old

Which one do you want to grow up to be?

If you repeatedly choose bondage or inaction, that pattern will, without question cost you your life. If repeated, over time it will ultimately cost you eternal rewards. A person who is unhealthy in spirit, soul, and body generally has an issue with the way they see taking action. It costs them happiness later by wanting to reap the wrong kind now.

Exercises

Today you are going to take one more step forward in your God-given freedom, away from bondage and comfort. This exercise is called "Free Your Mind". It's a very powerful exercise as long as you're honest with yourself and you keep writing. *This will allow you to quickly get rid of any areas of your life that are spreading you too-thin and taking you're eyes off of what is important.*

Let's go to 2 Timothy 2:16. This scripture is speaking of an outward babbling, confusion or ungodliness. We know a principle from the Bible that a person reflects their inner condition through their outer action. The idea behind this exercise is that we are going to cut right to the source of any confusion, fear, or inaction in your life.

If your home or office is disorganized and you can't find what's important, it makes it very hard to work on what's significant. Same thing goes with your mind. If your mind is disorganized and you always have things running around in it, if you have chatter filling your head, then you can't use time very efficiently because you're not thinking well.

Here's what you're going to do:

Write down everything that is on your mind RIGHT NOW … write down everything that you're thinking about … all your fears … worries … unanswered questions … aspirations … incomplete projects … random ideas … relationship situations … things you forgot earlier … every single thought that comes into your mind … all of it … take action … write down everything on your mind … write for 15, 30, 100 minutes straight, whatever it takes until you're mind is silenced.

Take action and GO, GO, GO. Come back when you're done, and continue from there. Stop reading and start writing NOW!

Okay, wow! I'm sure you wrote a ton of stuff. Isn't it amazing how many different things are running around our minds! So, now it's time for part two of the exercise. Let's go through your list.

- Circle everything that's within your ability to do something about (these are things that you can either individually or with someone's help, handle)
- Put a check-mark by everything that is outside your direct impact (these are things you will need to lift up to Christ in prayer)
- If it's just waaaay out of the park and you don't know why you were thinking about it, scribble it out and do your best to consciously let it go

Once you've done that.

- Take the items that you circled and put them in priority order (using the prioritization method from Chapter 1). These are the mental and physical areas that you are going to work on moving forward

- The other items, the ones with checks, make another list and you're going to lift them up to God in prayer. These are the spiritual areas you are going to submit to God.

Now you have your circles and checks. The circles will be **Your To-Do list** (with you being the action taker) and the checks will be your **Prayer list** (with God being the primary influencer).

This will allow for you to find clarity on the things you want to get off your mind and get into action. Once you've done this, you want to ask yourself one more question as you comb through the list just to make sure you got everything:

Is there anything in your life that you have a strong sense God wants you to do, but you haven't proceeded because of bondage, fear, or lack of faith?

Okay good, do this and take action on everything you can right now.

Key objectives from this chapter

Simplified your thought life

Prioritized what's important

Cleaned up any clutter

Chapter 3 – Direction

"Remember how short my time is ..."

Psalm 89:47 KJV

Picture this: What if Jesus just came down from heaven, was baptized by John … then just decided to hang out? Maybe start a couple carpentry projects … teach James to fish … get in all the experiences he could … not really tell anyone who he was … visit the Temple occasionally and shake a few hands … avoid the Pharisees …

Where would that leave you and I today?

What does this description bring to mind for you?

How does this compare to Acts 2:42-47?

The truth is Jesus was decisive, productive, and persuasive in compelling the world to his revelation. He wants this exact same type of advancement for you. He wants you to go into the world as a saint, a Christian, as someone made in the image of God - and to advance forward.

So let's start understanding what the Bible tells us about …

Directing Time

What men and women of every age and background have found so impactful about the inspired word of God is that it speaks as a historical document, a poetic text, and above all a clear path for life. We're going to use it as our dictionary today. No Websters!

Read Genesis 1:1. We can gather some compelling truth here:

- God exists outside of time

- He is the author of the realm

- We're the insiders

Have you ever …

… spent too much time on what's not important - only to find out it was too late to focus on what is?

… fallen asleep to feel like you've woken up minutes later refreshed?

… moved like lightning in an emergency and not knew how you did it?

Time is funny that way. Sometimes we feel like it's a straight line, but we have no clue. God can and will do what he wants with this realm that we exist in. Sometimes he shows us this in our lives, but we're just the vessels in the continuum.

Next, read Joshua 10:13-14 and ask … What does this say about God's sovereignty over time?

- That God has exercised his external authority over time

- That time benefits the righteous

- And even though we want Him to, this probably won't happen again because we're late for an important meeting or event or even if we pray really hard!

It's important to realize we have the ability to direct our choices ...
not God's

The freedom He's granted us is almost too big at times! We tend to shy back into repetition instead of moving forward in that freedom. That leads to anxiety and pressure. Right now is a time to realize that *your present situation can change tremendously through the powerful combination of God's will and your choices.*

Now read Ecclesiastes 3:1-8. What does this chapter add to the previous scripture?

- There are degrees of actions in life from excellent to poor

- We have many choices that are possible

- God's clear intent for us is to sow toward his identity, to be *and do* righteousness

Maybe you've made some poor choices or maybe there have been some external issues that have you caught up in a pace that's too fast. Regardless of the reason, **SO WHAT!** You are where you are and we know that God wants you to move forward making the best choices **STARTING NOW!** He wants you to get out of the trap and transform into the likeness of His image. He will calibrate your position like a navigation system and lead you from right where you are.

Let's visit the New Testament and read Romans 12:2

Do you see the pattern?

- God encourages us to use time well
- God tells us, now, to strive for His best
- God wants to see an outward sign of this … a transformation

This scripture isn't an option, it's a command! God didn't build us to be the same. God built us to *transform* into the likeness of Jesus. The scripture doesn't say," *conform to the world, stay the same, or transform … pick one.*" It says you are either moving backward toward the world or forward into the image of Christ … move forward.

Now read Hosea 10:12 and we'll reinforce the message:

Yet again:

- You're built to produce fruit
- You're meant to change for the better
- You will reap the benefits of the harvest!

The Bible's definition for time is:

A structure that God designed for us to honor Him and be fruitful within.

It's that simple. God is the author of order. He wants us to live a fruitful life dedicated to loving one another and living in righteousness. That's why He's painted eternity on our hearts and made us aware of His presence.

The Benefits of Using Time Wisely

So, with time defined, where do we go from here? We need to understand the benefit of time that we're looking for. Because time in and of itself is meaningless - unless there's something good we're going to do with it. This is key to uncover in your life because it takes life's focus and puts it in the right place.

As we talk about life and getting more of it, what are we really trying to accomplish? What do I really mean by that? I think what we're all looking for in life is to align with our true God-given freedom. We're all going after that feeling of freedom to do what's most important in our lives, right? To be able to do with time what is most beneficial.

Let's get right to the big picture and ask, *"Why are we trying to use time better?"* The reason has two parts. It's because we're trying to manifest that freedom and get out of the bondage that the world does it's best to place us in.

Guess what? The world gets in by allowing us to feel like we're "the same", "normal", or "not special". And that's one of the biggest lies a person can allow to get into their head. Here's why it's an effective lie for those who believe it. If a person thinks they're not special, they limit their ability to produce fruit and they seek either idleness or busyness. They put a glass ceiling on all of their undertakings in life and they only look to the sky for the pretty view instead of ways they can fly.

Scripture tells us we're unique and made *in the image of God.* Read Genesis 1:27. Then read Ecclesiastes 7:29. *What does the uniqueness of the image of God really mean?* The world will tell you *image* is about the way you look. The truth is the scripture is referring to the beauty of your internal virtue. The condition of your heart. The deceit of "being normal" keeps people from their true inward and outward potential in Jesus Christ and it keeps them trapped in themselves.

I bet you can find something special about everyone you know. In contrast, I bet they could find something special about you, too. It's when, in humility, you start to recognize your God-given uniqueness and abilities, that you can start really being effective in walking in the freedom God's given you.

Two Perspectives on Freedom

How does one walk in freedom? After studying the topic for a good amount of time I've found that freedom can be understood from a few perspectives. I believe there's inner freedom and outer freedom.

I can best describe inner freedom as something that boils down to our relationship with Jesus Christ, and the resounding, abundant, miraculous grace that He's provided us. You see, that's where most areas of our life go wrong, because they get rigid and lose their focus on Christ, they're more like a structure, *laws* or complication that doesn't tie back to the source.

Let's look at the second aspect of freedom. There's the outpouring of God's grace in the choices we make and the outcomes they give to both us and those around us. The feeling of the external freedom of love, achievement, efficiency or the lack thereof. When we don't have those two things running on all cylinders in our life, we don't feel as free as we can.

If our relationship with Christ isn't right and we're only achieving on the outside in our careers, we don't feel good about it. If we're fulfilled on the inside, but we aren't producing fruit outwardly in our families or communities then it's the same thing, we don't feel good about it. So, we're going to do our best to marry these two ideas in your approach to life.

Questions About Freedom

Read what Jesus says in John 8:31-32.

Now you can connect the dots from *time* to *freedom* to *truth*. Let's break down a few walls to feeling free *and being effective.*

- As Christians, do we fully rely on the Holy Spirit to guide us? Is that what God meant?

Or

- Do we prepare, plan and set a path? Is that self-interest?

Let's make something clear. God has predestined us for glory. Some of us, including myself, get caught up at times thinking God is looking down on us with a pair of balancing scales. That's just not true. For example, *"Does God want me to walk in faith right now or plan this out myself?"* Which one is in God's will?

Sometimes the truth of one biblical idea leads us to believe that anything outside of it wouldn't be true. Sometimes we mess up our own questions. We think answers have to be opposites when they are *"yes"* on both accounts. It's OK. We all do it.

I want to show you two scriptures - Romans 8:14 and 2 Timothy 4:1-2.

These scriptures are a basis for how we approach life. First by spirit, then by preparation. Throughout God's word we are encouraged to be led by the Spirit and to be prepared. We have to have this core understanding that there is a biblical call to use time wisely. It's repeated throughout His word. Just look up the words "order", "prepare", or "led" in your concordance if you have one. It will help to cement this idea for you.

You can see the trend of how God had order in creation, yet it was all spirit driven:

- Read the New Testament and the order of Christian Spiritual Virtues in 2 Peter 1:5-8

- If you look at the Feasts of the Old Testament and their order, there is a practical and spiritual significance to the life and times of Jesus Christ.

- If you can picture the order and spiritual importance of every single detail of the Tabernacle in the book of Exodus, from the oil to the incense there is a supernatural bond there. Yet, at the same time … there were practical expectations for those who watched over it.

Look at how focused Jesus' ministry was. Personally, I was confused when thinking too hard about walking in faith versus walking in my own will. I came to the conclusion that if I was trying to figure something out that should have been really simple, there had to be an author to the confusion. Confusion is exactly what your enemy wants. God's truth will break through and be clarified in simplicity. If you look at the meaning of the word "Abyss" which is used in conjunction with Hell, it's represented by disorder, chaos and confusion.

Here's the truth: *God is in you, and if you walk too much in your own will, He'll set you straight.*

Here's the main idea of this chapter:

Being led by the Holy Spirit *is* being prepared to do the will of God.

Here's another common question -

"What about Matthew Chapter 6 and the Sermon on the Mount, when Jesus spoke about not worrying about tomorrow, your clothes, what you will eat … your life?"

The answer is in the sermon itself. Jesus said not to *worry*. He didn't say not to look forward, get ready, or focus on what's to come. He actually said what to focus on in verse 33. Righteousness! As followers of Christ we have been set on the path of Righteousness. Look at Proverbs 4:18.

Don't worry, be righteous.

Psalm 49:5 let's us know there's already trouble here today. So, if you're going to worry – worry now – worry hard – worry as much as you possibly can! Get it all out! But, it's not what God wants. It won't get you anywhere either. Not worrying is freedom and truth and using your life wisely according to the Bible.

We're going to be using our understanding of God's view of freedom and truth to do our best to feel harmonized and balanced with that perspective. That internal sense of peace, Godly insight and making a difference for Jesus Christ in all areas of our life.

We're really going to aim to rounding out those areas so that when you get to the end of this process, you'll feel like you're more in-tune with time then you've ever been, as if you're an instrument playing the song that God intended and getting more results than you've ever gotten while tuning out all the worldly distractions.

Exercises

1. On a regular sized piece of paper, start by brainstorming and listing 6-8 areas of your life that are the *most important* for you and that align with God's intent for how your time should be used. Some ideas to do this are:

    - **Roles in life ...** for example:

      husband/wife, father/mother, manager

    - **Areas important to you ...** for example:

      financial freedom, physical health, or public service

    - **Your own mix of these or others**, reflecting the things that are your priorities in life like:

      humility, morality & purity, righteousness, family, health, spiritual fulfillment, love, relationships, patience, self-control, generosity, adventure, achievement, passion, creativity, leaving a legacy, fun/happiness, positive attitude, learning, helping others, simplicity, security, peace of mind, respect, gratitude, abundance, compassion, faith, growth, honesty, integrity, kindness, selflessness, significance, wisdom, peace

2. Rank the areas (1st, 2nd, 3rd ...) in order of their importance in your life.

3. Now based on a normal week or month, again, rank these areas (1st, 2nd, 3rd ...) based on the amount of time you commit to each.

4. Now look at the two rankings for each area. Do you see any big differences? Does your chart look and feel balanced? Do you think you are where you are supposed to be right now?

5. If you are out of balance in any given area, write down the next specific physical action you need to take in order to bring your life back on track.

Remember, a balanced life in harmony with Godly direction does not mean matching the ranks perfectly in each area. It might mean a slight adjustment or compromise based on what you sense God wants in your life.

Once you've completed this process, You should have your **direction** in question #1, you will have **a method for looking at the big picture** in questions 2 and 3, and you will have **a way to find direction, balance, and priorities** in questions 4 and 5.

Key objectives from this chapter

Understand the theme of time using the Bible

Find out how God wants you to balance your time

Figure out the steps and adjustments

Chapter 4 – Prioritized Action

"Do not merely listen to the word, and so deceive yourselves. Do what it says."
James 1:22

When I was a boy, my grandmother had quite a few trees in her yard. My favorite was her fig tree because it was the best to climb. Now, as I look back, it seemed like whenever I would go to her house there were ripe figs ready to pluck from the branches. I would run up the trunk and use the front of my shirt to collect the little purple fruit. Then I'd eat my fill, pour the rest into the fruit basket, and play for the rest of the day. It's amazing how that tree left such a memory in my life because of it's fruit.

In sharing that story, there's an important parallel to our lives in Christ. Let's look at Matthew chapter 13:3-9 and 18-23. Here, Jesus gives us one of the main priorities in our Christian life: *Productivity*. One distinction of being a follower of Christ is *"fruit"*. In this parable, Jesus gave us some fundamental guidance when it comes to the challenges of bearing fruit in life.

1. Our Enemy
2. Trouble & Persecution
3. Worry & Money

Our Enemy

As Satan tries to fight against us, he already knows that he can't have your soul. It's important to recognize that as a Christian, you have already won the eternal war against him through Jesus Christ. His goal today is for your earthly life to fail so you can't impact the lives of others. As Christians, we shouldn't focus on what's already done or pay much attention to someone who doesn't deserve our attention. Instead we can be wise to his methods used in order to avoid them. Through Jesus you have authority. It's important to understand this position. Read Ephesians 2:6.

Here's an important revelation: once you realize you have been set apart, set above, and are destined for righteousness, regardless of what is set in front of you, the negative conditions around you get smaller and the positive influences start becoming more and more visible. Spiritually you are coming from a position of authority in the matters of this world! Spiritually, you reside OVER the matters that sometimes seem like walls you can't climb.

Trouble and Persecution

Regarding trouble and persecution, here's a parallel scripture that's not pointed out too often. Read 2 Timothy 3:12. Did Paul really say that? Man … I thought being a Christian would open up some magical floodgates where God would bless my lottery tickets and everyone at church would like me? Did I sign up for the wrong small group?

Sometimes the grandness of God leads us to have questions about hard times. It's normal. The Bible says … this life might just be hard … no promises of earthly prosperity from Paul or the

Holy Spirit here. This scripture tells us we can't avoid persecution. The big hint is that we've found the method to overcome persecution. That method is always through Jesus Christ. The message is reinforced in Philippians 4:12.

Worry and Money

Sometimes worry acts like a false comforter. We feel that if something is occupying our attention then it's a good thing. That's not true … we can see the fruit of worry in the parable. Here's a further truth about worry that will help you to minimize it:

- It's always based in the future
- It's always based on uncertainty

Worry is in stark opposition to faith

As you read Hebrews 11:1 you can understand we have a choice to make here. If you can develop your spiritual senses, accept in your heart that Jesus died to give us the faith for today, then you can build up your confidence in how you approach the emotions and conflicts that come up in your daily life. Look at 2 Corinthians 1:3-4.

If we're too worried about managing our own affairs, then we can't move on to the big picture and start helping others in their lives. *That's where the enemies strategy lies. He wants you to be ineffective in your life and for Christ.*

Then, there's money. We think," *What does God want me to do with my finances?"* Then we end up turning inward to ourselves for answers, and the unproductive cycle repeats ...

Money can be an idol or a tool for effectiveness

We realize that our finances help advance the Gospel message. What's great is that we can understand both the system of this world and God's requirements for financial obedience. One of our enemy's tricks is to keep financial situations private so Christians are confused and don't advance financially or those who are prospering in God's will get caught in financial disobedience. In God's eyes $100 from the heart is more than $10,000 from the hip. Read 2 Chronicles 31:5 from the Old Testament and 2 Corinthians 9:7 from the New Testament.

It's important to keep money in an appropriate place in your life. The Federal Reserve Bank of Chicago defines money as," ... *the confidence people have that they will be able to exchange such money for other financial assets and for real goods and services whenever they choose to do so"*. Our confidence in Christ should be first and foremost over all other things yet we should value the resources and honor God with what he has given us stewardship over.

In the book of Acts Chapter 5, after Jesus was resurrected and taken back up to heaven, Peter was confronted with a situation where a husband and wife, Ananias and Sapphira, had sold some land and put money before God. Peter didn't have to do anything to resolve it because the Holy Spirit convicted their hearts so severely, they died on the spot. They had their relationships mixed up. At the same time a lack of material resources should not diminish a person's confidence in Christ. Look at the confidence of Peter with empty pockets in Acts 3:6!

If we have our biblical priorities aligned, the results will bear fruit in our lives. Those things that are getting in the way (evil, trouble and persecution, uncertainty and money) will be more recognizable and easier to overcome.

As you look to scripture and the parable of the seed and the sower, you can understand that God has an intention behind your design. He's given you a list of obstacles. He influences his character by wanting you to …

… have deep roots

… and bear fruit

The Application for Today

When Jesus walked the earth, the condition was much different than it is today. There were no car loans, cell phones, or corporations. Through the course of history, people are becoming more and more inundated by society and the things going on around us, versus the spiritual realm that we sometimes forget controls everything.

The current of world information is flowing faster and faster. This flow somewhat indoctrinates us to the world instead of to God. It tries to grab our attention and redirect it. Let's face it, most people today are visual so, to some, Jesus is just a story and a God they can't see. But we can't let the pace of culture rob us or them of the truth and our intended fruit in life.

Remember back when we talked about wisdom, knowledge and information? The question for you is, *should cultural information rock your boat?*

Now re-read Matthew 8:18-27. Pause and think about the idea it conveys to you today about what God intends for you.

The wisdom of Jesus never fades. Culture may change, we may gain more data and information. All it will serve to do is magnify the words of Jesus from the simplest situations to the biggest challenges.

As a Christian, it's our duty to have a clear distinction between those things that are profitable in our lives and those that aren't. The way we do that is by looking at the world's landscape through a biblical lens. The first step is realizing it's okay to filter your time and your life and there is an order to the madness that sometimes consumes us. Here's how it goes:

1. Seek God as soon as the issue arises
2. Seek the eternal wisdom of the Bible
3. Seek support from Godly peers
4. Act biblically

It's simple to apply –

Example:

Let's say someone has too much unproductive communication wasting their time.

Possible Solution:

1. *Intentionally pray and look to the Bible*

2. *God's word says to avoid busyness*

3. *Find out the best ways to approach the situation based on people who are in similar situations*

4. *Keep your heart in the right place. Keep the cell phone on quiet so it doesn't interrupt. Have filters on your life so you pay attention to what's important. Check messages when necessary. Don't focus on tasks of little value. Keep focus items top of mind and in conversations.*

Pretty clean and orderly, right? Just as God wants our lives to be.

Priority 2 – *Self-control*

Next, have you ever noticed the Bible never refers to time management? The challenge of our lives is to focus on the right things and get them done. It says the days are evil in Ephesians … In Proverbs 27:1 we get this theme as well … and in James 4:13-15 it repeats the message.

Steven Covey and David Allen are both leaders in the field of productivity. They agree that the real challenge in life is *self-management*, what we think, and most importantly what we do, even though most of the products that they offer are in the field of *"time management"*…

Here's why, when you try to manage and focus on something outside yourself, you project focus incorrectly. We don't have any control over it. If you say, *"I want to manage X better"*, you're going to realize it's like trying to organize the water in the ocean, it can't be done. You can be doing something more productive.

Here's an important realization I had: If instead, you would say," *I want to learn how to understand myself, my nature, and my interactions"* that creates a whole new perspective.

So what do I mean there? When you say you want to manage X, it's an outward thing. You're externalizing. When you say, *"I'm going to manage myself"* you're taking responsibility for what you're doing and for the results you're getting. It places the focus on *"why"* instead of *"how"* and the true reason behind results starts to surface.

There's a funny character in the book of Proverbs called "the sluggard". He's the epitome of sloth and what not to do. No self-control. Like the Homer Simpson of the Bible.

Read Proverbs

- 6:6
- 13:4
- 20:4
- 26:15

The struggles of life can be overcome by getting better control of yourself. When you realize this, it points your spiritual antenna in the right direction. The only way you can do this is to come closer to God. Then, when you start to develop self-control and discipline, you become more of a disciple ... hence the word.

I was talking with a friend and we thought about how the ministry of Jesus lasted only three years, yet the impact of what his grace did for our lives will last forever. Look at how he mastered the world, his spirit, soul, and body in order to accomplish so much in such a short time! Bottom line, focus on self-control.

One of the most eye-popping principles I've learned is: *self-control is hard!* We think we're already in control, or we can buy control, or it's easy. You can challenge this principle yourself. Try to hire someone to manage your time and see what kind of progress *you* make … fast for 24 hours and see how you're not in control … switch from watching television to reading the Bible and learn how it takes discipline … or when you wake up, make the effort to sit up and have both of your feet hit the floor automatically - forever. These things require a conscious effort and your mind and body will rebel.

The good news is you can learn to manage these self-control disciplines better. Read Galatians 5:22-26. You can learn to control, conquer, and have authority over your body by the renewing of your mind and engaging with your spirit. It's very important that you realize a good portion of life is about self-control and self control is hard.

Priority 3 – *Alignment*

As a Christian, you are constantly aligning with God's will. Since the beginning of recorded history, man has been on a quest to figure himself out. From Aristotle and the Greeks to you and I as Christians. If you happen to do some research in this area you'll realize man has always been trying to dig into the details. It's kind of like reverse engineering the human puzzle.

As we find out more information about ourselves, it's interesting to see how the Bible stands the test of time. You see, God didn't give us a detailed blueprint of creation, but we are able to understand the framework for how we're made. Things like spirit, soul, and our physical-self from Genesis 2:7.

We are made uniquely to look up to God, reach out to mankind, and interact in the world

Our spirit is the seat of our *God knowledge*, faith, and worship. Our soul is where our emotions, logic, and memories reside and connect with who *we* are. Our physical self is how we connect with *the world* through our senses.

Sometimes as people, we have the illusion that we're only aligned with one or two of these areas and the others don't matter. The reality is that our entire being is made up of an intricate puzzle that works best when all of the pieces are put together to form the picture that God has intended for us. One of the enemy's strategies is division. That division includes dividing you internally so you don't feel like who you were intended to be.

Your advantage is in God and your relationship with Jesus. This distinction will drive your life. On the other hand, when we close up to who God is, it can chisel away at who we are as people and damage our soul. If we neglect our physical body we weaken our soul into thinking that we are not miraculously created as the Bible tells us we are. *That's the enemy at work.*

Now what's weird is that we can live seemingly functional lives as this happens, but we can't *live out* everything that God has for us unless we are using all He's given us. You'll notice that when you're jammed-up in life and you're having trouble moving forward, it's usually because some of your pieces are missing. You may be physically pulled to do something but you know spiritually that you shouldn't do it, that's *you* in turmoil and that's where a lot of our inner conflict comes from.

In Acts 17:18 Paul was speaking to a group of Epicurean and Stoic philosophers in Athens. The Stoics were philosophers who shut down their emotions in favor of trying to reason God. The Epicureans were disciples of Epicurus, who before he died, gave up on the idea that one could be a Stoic and just decided to, "Eat, drink and be merry." Neither of these two approaches work in life. They just cause internal struggle. Jesus wants us to use all of our available pieces and complete the puzzle of life.

If you understand that as a Christian, you already have a huge advantage at being productive and managing yourself … getting the most out of life becomes a lot easier.

Priority 4 – *Embrace Positive Change*

We have what you could think of as *highways* we develop inside ourselves. You might think of these on three levels - as your spirit, soul, and physical *highways*. There are different factors to consider from who we are to who we surround ourselves with. Some are inside and some are outside.

One of the clearest images of this is in Proverbs chapter 3, written in the 10th century B.C. It shows the clear paths between the spirit, soul, and body and why seeking God first is the only answer in life. Read that scripture … then, let's look with fresh eyes to Romans 12:2.

If you do something out of repetition for a while you get into a pattern and you won't be able to change it automatically. Patterns don't change overnight and change is hard. In contrast to that, with the power of God, we can overcome natural tendencies and build new paths of self-control.

Spirit

When we accept Jesus Christ into our life it opens up a door. That door closes those behind us and opens others in front of us. It turns on a light that is brighter than 10,000 suns and whiter than the whitest white that compels our lives to reach out in intentional devotion, unmerited giving and loving favor for all in this world, just like Jesus.

This highway is what causes people to loose chemical addictions, mend relationships and cause physical healing to occur. Transformation of the spirit is the saving grace of Jesus and the guiding light behind transformation of the soul and body.

Increase your soul caliber

In several scriptures, the Bible tells us that our thoughts bring actions. It took scientists a while to find this out but they finally caught up. In the brain, there is a process called myelination. When your brain thinks a thought over and over again, each time it produces a chemical called myelin. It's a coating that makes it easier for a thought to form the next time. That's why studying for a test works, because you have a myelin highway. It's literally like putting smooth pavement on a road and it builds up a neural connection so that it becomes easier and more natural to think a thought.

In terms of emotions: they're stimulating to us, even when they're negative. They act like habit forming chemicals. What we find is that emotions can be just like thoughts. We can recognize our emotions and what they bring into our lives. We can also allow our emotions to be triggered for us. Someone helping or hindering us can cause a reaction that isn't thought about … it's triggered.

Thinking a productive thought makes it easier to think again and then to act without thinking in the future. This is why it is always hard to do something new for about the first month or so, but as time goes by, change becomes much easier. That is why it is so important to capture every thought for Christ.

Physical Self

The same thing goes for our body. You have muscle memory. If you go through a movement over and over it's as if you're paving a road. It becomes natural. Whether you're stagnant or active, both cause you to add more of the same to your life.

Now as you open up to the previous principle of the different puzzle pieces we are made of, and how these different parts perform better as they act together, you'll notice that most of what you do is habitual. It will awaken you to where you need to connect your parts, build some new roads, and direct traffic.

God created some key systems within you and I. As we advance in our learning and find out more about the intricacies of His design, there's some common sense that we often overlook! Today's world works against our design. If we get sick, we pop pills. We try not to cry because it's not considered status quo. We're tired because we don't sleep enough, so we offset fatigue with caffeine.

Sometimes we feel like there is a great secular divide between the world today and God's wisdom. That's when people start dying . . . refusing to go to a doctor because they were waiting on God's healing. The men of Issachar were a critical part of David's team. They were men who knew the times. Read 1 Chronicles 12:32. As long as the lens of the Bible is used for clarity, you can come to a good understanding of what's in tune and what's out of tune with true wisdom in today's world.

At the same time, the Bible inspires us to *right action*. We all have times when we feel like we're riding (or even laying on) a hamster wheel. It's okay, it happens to us all. The point is, the Bible has all the answers to get back up and running. There are some key insights in the word that help us get over any barriers in those times we lack desire.

Solomon tells us that too much learning is unfruitful. At times, Jesus went off alone in order to pray. If you're ever stuck, at work, for example, and you can't get that idea for the project you've been working on, take a break and do something that refreshes you on another level (spiritually, physically, emotionally . . .). You could listen to worship music at lunch ... work-out ... talk to your spouse ... a co-worker ... read a fiction novel ... write down your feelings about your favorite scripture … remember back to a breakthrough point in your life. It's biblical.

Priority 5 – *Prayer*

Making room for a regularly scheduled time almost feels like an act of internal rebellion at first. It seems backwards to realize that in order to get more done I need to stop what I'm doing and reflect. My regular time with God changes, becoming more focused. It's not the importance of the routine or ritual, but the importance of the obedience and thoughtful seeking of God to answer the questions that I can't. Time focused on God is not just an interruption in my day, but a reminder that all time is God's. I prefer to pray upon waking and during the day I have conversations with God. Let's look at the importance of prayer in our life. Turn to 1 Peter 4:7 and read.

If you have struggles inside, you're going to have conflict on the outside, but prayer is your weapon. Open, honest, forthright prayer. Prayer is a meeting with God. Knowing the presence of God is your birthright. *Not the act of praying itself, but communion with your creator.* This is important to take in. Otherwise prayer becomes religion.

Martin Luther has a quote that goes, *"I have so much to do (today) that I should spend the first three hours in prayer."*

What you want to do is realize how much conflict you have on the inside and how you can start to release that and give it up to God so that you can have less struggle inside and out.

A. W. Tozer wrote, *"What comes into your mind when you think about God is the most important thing about you."*

It's about releasing the struggles you can't and weren't meant to handle. Praying is about letting go of the troubles of this world in the name of Jesus Christ, who gave you authority. It allows you to focus. It opens the curtain to what sometimes escapes you. It even attracts money and makes you more attractive to others. *(Just kidding … making sure you're focused!)*

In truth, prayer allows for you to act on what's important in life.

God's given a front-stage and a back-stage to just about everything. If you look at performing arts as an example. It takes a lot of preparation before the show in order to be ready for opening night, which occurs in front of a live audience. Nothing would come together unless there was a screenwriter who authored it all, people designing the set, and lots of communication beforehand.

With you, the big show is your life and you're on an even bigger stage than Broadway. Yet sometimes we fail to make the unseen preparations that make for a fantastic performance. Sometimes we need to remember that there is always a camera running and we're the star of the screen.

Connecting with the author *beforehand* is key.

Sometimes, *you must slow down* in order to speed up.

Priority 6 – *Recognize Opportunities*

Next, let's look at how the Bible tells us to focus on opportunities. Go to Ephesians 5:15-16.

In life, there are only a few things that really matter. When Jesus walked the earth, he focused on the two biggest opportunities he could.

1. Providing eternal life
2. Setting a perfect example

Because we don't focus on the important things, we don't advance in our lives. The bottom line is: You don't want to just focus on what's important, *you want to focus on the biggest opportunities and make them your priorities.* There's a difference. In Acts 6:2-4 The Apostles understood this ...

Waiting tables is important for some people, there is an opportunity there, but not for the Apostles. Many of us have waited tables at one point or another in our lives. The Apostles biggest opportunity was in their ministry of sharing the gospel. When we waste ourselves on things outside of our gifts, talents and direct abilities, like the busyness or mundane things that trickle in every day, we don't make the progress that we were designed for. That's where we stumble.

When you focus on opportunities, you're able to direct your attention on what God wants you to change in the world. This is where you will make the biggest difference in your life and in the lives of others. Whether it is waiting on tables, running your business or in ministry. Where you focus your freedom is almost as important as where you focus your faith.

Keep in mind the previous 5 priorities because they build on each other. You want to get multiplied leverage as these ideas compound.

Priority 7 – *Become Like Christ*

The last priority we're going to discuss is your freedom in Christ. So, God wants you to be productive in this life. He's created you in His image and has allowed us to realize that in His perfect design there are change mechanisms that lead you toward the order, productivity, and transformation that he ultimately has planned for your success. He's even given you a direct up-link to Him through prayer to discern where you should exercise your will.

What's next?

For some people, from tomorrow on, their day might be an extension of their past. The same things they did and the same things that happened yesterday may be what they get today and tomorrow. In fact, they don't even see any options in the future except for what they did yesterday. It's because, they feel they don't have a frame of reference and they've never known anything else. That's true of everyone.

If we've never seen a certain type of food, for example and then we see someone eating this dish at a restaurant, we're not going to recognize it at first. We might get hungry or repulsed, depending on what it is. If we don't know what to look for, we might overlook it on the menu. Some might become curious about it and even try it, but if you're not familiar with something, then you're not going to easily identify with it.

That's why we have Jesus. To overcome by example ...

If you take a biblical perspective to life and say, *"I'm not going to live out more of my past or who I was, but focus on Christ and live a future created and exampled by him."* It instantly changes your entire life. Tomorrow can be the same or it can be the moment everything changes.

Most people like to hold on to who they feel they are. They like to hold on to their story, their excuses and things they do to get approval from others. The truth is, everyday you're losing some old you. Your memory fades and your looks deteriorate. What really is there to hold on to ... of you?

Let's Look to God speaking through the Prophet Isaiah in 43:18-19. If you try to hold on to the old you, you can't become Christ-like. If you try to hold on to your old ways, there is no way you can develop into the person that Christ has called you to be ... Let it go ... You must walk-out into the future that's waiting for you.

Exercises

1. Based on the direction you uncovered in Chapter 3, what specific priorities do you sense God has for your life? 1,3, and 5 years from now? Write them out.

2. What are the actions you will take in order to achieve these priorities ... today ... this week ... this month ...

3. Set a date on the calendar 3 months from now when you will revisit the questions in this chapter to review your progress.

4. How can you exercise more self-control in your life daily?

5. What outside influences are causing bad habits that rob you of time, energy, or value in your life right now?

6. Today you're going to build a habit. Before you go to bed, challenge yourself to write out the most important items to get accomplished the next day. Then pray about what God wants you to focus on that week. As you complete these daily items, you're keeping an agreement with yourself and prompting you're daily direction to be committed to God's will. This will act as a reinforcement to help you really think about what's important a day in advance and help you get it done. You can also look back later and see how much more you've accomplished by doing this!

    (Note: It's important to know that you're not a machine. This habit won't come easily, I promise! The importance here is to do your best, feel good about it, and make progress!)

Key objectives from this chapter

> *Understood the 7 biblical priorities*
>
> *Connected yesterday's ideas with today's*
>
> *Action!*

Chapter 5 – Reduction

"In a large house there are articles not only of gold and silver, but also of wood and clay; some are for noble purposes and some for ig-noble."
2 Timothy 2:20

A revelation that completely changed my life was grasping the need for people in today's world to re-evaluate their resources. We've accumulated so much, yet we've gained so little as a people. Our standard of life is at it's ceiling but our quality of life is on the floor. In a day when wants overcome needs and then overshadow purpose … it's time to simplify.

If you look back at the life of Jesus, he was able to overshadow and enthrall the world with minimal resources in a short amount of time by leveraging the three resources contained in the following pages. It's a must that you have these resources present in your life. Furthermore, it's a must that you reduce anything that is taking away from them as quickly as possible in order to live a biblically productive life.

One of the things that stuck with me from being in the military was that in an environment like boot-camp … it didn't matter:

- Where you came from

- who could make the best excuses

- or what someone thought about you

It did matter however …

- how resourceful you were with what you had

- how much discipline you were willing to receive & exercise

- and how well you worked with others for the mission

Another thing you realize is that the weeds of life grow automatically, every day, and you must be able to tend to the health of your own garden before you can tend to the weeds of others. That's where leaders are identified in the military. You must acquire the resources that allow for you to keep your garden growing without having to tend it all the time. Then you've got to learn how to skip over all of the messes in order to accomplish the mission.

In the same sense, boot camp strips away the unnecessary elements of the world and brings out our core resources. They are:

- Identity

- Communication

- and Influence

Identity

Who are you? Everyone has a distinct uniqueness about them because God breathed us into being. The condition of that uniqueness is up to us. You can have a healthy identity based on the image and true biblical character of God and the way it reflects back on you.

Read Matthew 16:13 and John 18:33-38, then read John 14:6. How does Jesus answer the question of his own identity? In life, action, and change! When Pilate asks him about his label Jesus dismisses it and gives Pilate the mission.

If you try to define yourself outwardly it often leads to regret. We are designed to live as God's children finding our way by his will. Unless we define our identity first by our relationship with Christ, we will encounter problems in our life. Knowing we are secure in Jesus gives us the confidence to truly be who we were created to be. The Holy Spirit then allows us to discover our gifts. Our identity "in Christ" is emphasized over and over in Scripture. Read John 1:12, 15:16, Colossians 2:9-10, Philippians 3:20, and 1 Peter 2:9.

Other people, the media, Satan, your experiences, and even your own thoughts sometimes will tell you many different lies about who you are and what you were put here to do. That's why you must believe God's intent for your life. Be aware of your thoughts. As you distinguish the lies, replace them with truth.

Ask God how you should act on your identity. This includes two parts: saying no to the pattern of sin, and choosing God's will. Don't live as a spiritual orphan, trying to find your security and significance through people, accomplishments, or possessions. As a believer in Jesus, you are a child of the Most High God.

What if you had something new and exciting that never got old? What if the excitement of new ideas and fresh opportunities continued forever? Guess what? That's what your identity in Christ is like. It never gets old because you are focused on the eternal God who is **the source of new life.** This means that you and I have already become a part of this **mission.** And your identity can reflect that.

Communication

How well do you play with others? We all have the ability to communicate. We all start with the very basic relationships in life —those with our parents and siblings. We then make certain decisions to grow and expand those relationships, and to seek new communication avenues with other people.

The first rule of communication I learned in the military was *"Message sent is not message received"*. That's why communication is an important area to understand. I know I'm not the only one who's tried to swallow words after they were let loose in a conversation. Unbridling your tongue can be the most challenging thing you do. On the other hand, you may talk more than you listen! Regardless, you might not realize how much people are really absorbing the words you say and walking them out in their lives. Let's look at some examples of these from Scripture.

Read the book of Acts, chapter 2 verses 14-47.

Peter had a strong, **direct** and assertive method of communicating. In this sermon on the day of Pentecost, Peter didn't hold back; he delivered a cutting message. And 3,000 people responded. He told the Jews who gathered they had *murdered* the true Messiah, and if they wanted to avoid the wrath of God they must *repent.*

When Jesus walked the earth, he veiled certain truths in **parable** form. Read Luke 15:3-7. Jesus understood that explicit truth isn't sweet music to all ears. Simply put, there were those who didn't have interest in God, but He was able to get His message in regardless.

Let's break down this parable and see what his real meaning was:

"Which of you men, if you had one hundred sheep, and lost one of them, wouldn't leave the ninety-nine in the wilderness, and go after the one that was lost, until he found it?"

Jesus speaks twice to the hearts of men here. First he says, *"Do you care enough about your fellow man to go against the norms?".* Secondly, He says, *"God cares about each single person enough to seek them out until they are his."*

"When he has found it, he carries it on his shoulders, rejoicing. When he comes home, he calls together his friends and his neighbors, saying to them, 'Rejoice with me, for I have found my sheep which was lost!"

Next, Jesus says,*"I am so excited when even one of my children comes back!"*

"I tell you that even so there will be more joy in heaven over one sinner who repents, than over ninety-nine righteous people who need no repentance."

And then, Jesus explains the wisdom of the parable.

On the other side, can we communicate effectively without emotion? Remember Acts 17 and the philosophers from Chapter 4? Today there are plenty of men who hide their emotions from God. With this in mind, we can understand the **logical** communication approach and our limitations. A key reason why men, to this very day, reject Jesus Christ is because they don't open their hearts. We need to be able to appeal to what they do have open to Christ in order to love them and draw them closer to Him.

Now Read Acts 17:22-34. You can see here that when *only* reason is used, the Bible doesn't call it intelligence, it calls it ignorance. There are plenty of reasonable Christians but they are followers with open minds *and hearts*. Logic is a starting point for a renewed understanding with the Greeks in Acts 17. Paul spoke to their ignorance and we can see the few that responded. Reasoning will bring the mind to Christ but full understanding comes from belief and *you cannot reason belief*, otherwise you will be caught in a trap of being reasoned out of it.

Let's look to the story of the blind man in John chapter 9. When someone really changes your life, it's impossible to hold it in or deny it, even under the most excruciating circumstances. You can't downplay the changes that occur today, you must challenge those who don't believe because of the changes that have occurred in your life. Additionally, if you know someone who has changed their life, it's just as difficult to hold it in. Look to scripture and the example of the Samaritan woman at the well in John chapter 4.

The book of James speaks of works. It tells us about the grace we have in front of God and how we should show that to men by what we do. This method of communication, some say, is the most powerful of all because what we do, **our choices**, the effects we have on the world, determine who we are. Look at Mother Theresa and the lifestyle she led or how about the Apostles? How about some examples from your own life? The power of action always reaches the hardest to reach people.

You can also find a contrast to the Stoics in **emotional** Christianity. It appeals only to the emotion. It doesn't engage the mind and is sometimes void of salvation, but God never intended for our emotions to be placed first in the order of our being. God intended for us to be spiritual beings and spirit comes from truth and truth comes from revelation, which is not an emotion.

Influence

How persuasive can you be? How much can you give positive change to others? Do they want more? Even if it seems like just a little bit. Jesus taught that the way we impact others is a reflection of our inward moral condition in Matthew 12:34-37. We can be secure in our identity as Christians and the change we have to offer to others in Jesus Christ. Influence is where we take our identity, add the ability to communicate, and put them together into a package of how we best impact the world.

Jesus defined influence … we can model our relationships from his. He was the most influential being to set foot on this earth. Today would be drastically different if Jesus had never communicated change into our lives. His steps were few, yet they left behind giant imprints.

Did you know that one of the main tenets of Christianity is a powerful part of influence. It's also one of the hardest parts. It's called **other orientation**. Read James 2:8. This gives us the foundation for a huge concept of influence. It's the concept that people are more willing to do something because they have been done for. To top it off, the Bible teaches not to expect any-thing in return, God will take care of that. It's a way of showing people that you can be trusted in a world where trust is lacking. As a Christian Jesus gave not to receive, but just to give. It's one of the most compelling truths revealed to mankind about growth.

The fact is, the Bible tells us the *real* disciples were not only influ-ential, but also **committed**. From that dedication, they bore eternal fruit in the lives of others and left a unique legacy all their own. That type of faith brings influence through action. Read 2 Timothy 4:10. Where do you think Demas' commitment was?

But influence is a two way street. You are either being influenced or being influential. To go along with that idea, there has been an interesting switch that has occurred over the last 20 years that is influencing many Christians in an unhealthy direction.

We've moved from God's abundance to a mentality of scarcity thinking.

In the world, people find objects and opportunities more attractive to the degree that they are scarce. Precious gems, one-day sales, even information that is scarce is more appealing. Yet, at the same time, there's an inconsistency between understanding God's abundance for our lives and the scarcity of resources that people truly don't understand because there's been a switch. The world has influenced people into thinking true happiness comes from the scarcity of God and the abundance of resources.

Read John 6:1-21. These are two stories with one theme. Jesus was testing Phillip and the disciples. Do we lean toward scarcity or the abundance of God? I can be sensitive to Philip's reaction in the first story. Simply, they were low on food with too many guests. I've been in similar situations (but with fewer guests of course). He didn't want to face 5000 hungry people. Philip was wrapped in scarcity. There wasn't enough. He looked at a situation in terms of what was missing, not the abundance that God could provide. What do you think would have happened to Phillip if he didn't have Jesus with him and he tried to lean on his own resources for the answer?

Scarcity is also the theme of the second story. The scarcity of faith. In the Army there's a saying," *There are no atheists in a fox-*

hole." That means when the storms of life go far beyond our ability to cope, we look to God, even if we deny it. When the tides are high and the waves are crashing, it tests our ability to look up or look down. Sailing on the ocean in a storm can be fear-provoking. It's in moments like these that you find out you're not as big or as capable of *survival* as you thought apart from God.

These stories are about God's abundance in the midst of scarcity. The disciples had listened to and saw miracles, yet Jesus knew the important lesson here. God is an abundant provider and in today's materialistic society we need to come to a complete un-derstanding of abundance and scarcity. Read Ezekiel 16:49. True scarcity, which can sometimes be thought of as discipline, has it's place. Look at the life of John the Baptist.

Think about what it means to be a follower of Christ and to rise up and influence that to others through your life? You might have to re-align your resources and invest more attention in the areas that matter eternally. You might have to challenge your current understanding of true abundance and focus your actions on how to share it. There are many things in life we can't control, including the mentality of others, but we can control how we re-spond to the rest of the world. Looking at things with a scarcity mentality is only productive if it's in line with God's abundance.

The Challenges

How we use these resources is incredibly important. There are simple things we can do with those basic resources: **Leverage, use**, and **abuse**. You have a choice.

1. Leverage

If you leverage something, there is a measurable benefit to the Kingdom of Jesus Christ. Whether it's leveraging your personality to reach someone, giving your gifts to others, building a relationship or otherwise.

2. Use

If you use a certain resource, you get little or nothing in return. If you spend most of your life watching television, you get little return, even if you get some brief intellectual stimulation from a show, it isn't terribly significant. For the most part, you get nothing in return for that time. It is used and gone. Maybe you squandered time complaining to others. There may be a little emotional satisfaction as you complain, but it doesn't amount to much and it might influence others to be complainers as well.

3. Abuse

If you abuse a resource, you get absolutely nothing in return. Waiting for things that aren't important amounts to an abuse of life. The same goes for blame. Blaming is simply an excuse for you to under-perform and fail. It is a complete abuse of identity, communication and influence. You can even abuse *leverage*. You may have *leverage* in life but do nothing with it.

The Choices

Others don't make these choices for you; it's up to you to proactively decide. Most people let others decide what they do with their resources and then regret decisions they make. They view the glass as half empty. This impacts their identity.

Since your identity is the lens through which you see the entire world, poor identity can greatly affect every aspect of your life. You have resources available to you and it's up to you to maximize and grow them. Don't make excuses for not doing so. You have to change your perspective.

Understand that you have enough resources to get started. You have everything you need to begin your journey. From this point on, move forward with the best days of your life. Understand this on all levels. If you operate from this viewpoint, you will reap the benefits. Everything has a resource and choice attached to it. There is no escaping that. The choices you make determine your life. If you are resourceful, you will choose wisely.

Exercises

In the previous chapters you've been equipped with the tools to make progress in your life (i.e. organize, prioritize, find clarity, balance, encourage action) *Answer questions 1 and 2* then find ways you can transition from Abusing to Using to Leveraging *using the tools to help answer question 3, 4, and 5.*

1. In three sentences or less. Who are you?

2. How can you enhance your communication productivity?

3. How can you exert more influence for Jesus Christ?

4. What areas of your life can use reduction and simplification?

5. What areas of your life will you re-align your mentality of scarcity and abundance?

6. How can you put together a plan to leverage your true resources?

Take what you've invested today and drill down on what these questions mean to you personally. Hopefully, you've realized that the key revolves around understanding ourselves and our actions for God.

Keep in mind that it's not really the day to day structures we put in place. The management structure for our life is us. Life is ultimately about you and I. The better questions we can ask ourselves, the better we can approach each day with clarity and freedom to make progress in what's most important.

This chapter and it's exercises should give you a kind of behind-the-scenes understanding. This is where you're starting to really hone in on the discovery that how we use our time is less and less about what you're doing and more and more about who you are and what you can become.

> ### Key objectives from this chapter
>
> *Reflection*
>
> *An analysis of your resources*
>
> *Simplification and reduction of clutter*

Chapter 6 – Conflicts

"My people are destroyed from lack of knowledge."

Hosea 4:6

Let's talk about a few trends that have happened over the last century that challenge our ability to best discern God's direction for us. We're going to focus on cultural conflicts and the emerging patterns of modern life. These trends are so quickly building and encroaching on our lives that we have to come to a place of understanding with them.

There are huge risks with living in today's modern world. These risks cause people to die young with stress filled lives or in contrast, live hollow long lives. Most of the risks people face in seeking God can be negated by focusing in on the primary danger we need to avoid in the first place.

The danger is that modern culture is stealing people from God

The good news is that we can take initiative and provide direction.

Conflict 1 - Information

The first conflict is a loss of wisdom. When it comes to the practical daily pieces of our lives, there's been a loss of wisdom.

In the information age, where e-mails travel faster than sound advice, it's easy to get caught up in trends, philosophy or approaches that don't last. They are fleeting like a breeze. That's why it's crucial for you to be grounded in your faith, so when the tide comes in, you can be confident in where you stand. Without wisdom, we waste opportunities and focus on ourselves or activities that have little or no value.

Today, we have plenty of information, some knowledge and even less available wisdom when it comes to every area of our daily lives. Culture has become obsessed with too much segmented information. In a fast paced culture, today's information is packaged in little bite-sized consumables so people can grab a bit here and a bit there. The problem comes in when you try to tie all of those bits together.

We've gone from a people who were driven by timeless Godly wisdom to a society that's settled for secular and segmented information. If you notice on television, news spots are being condensed. On the internet, video clips are getting shorter. In life, careers are almost a thing of the past …

There is a cultural system of conscious sleep, and I want you to be awake for everything you will engage with in your life. We need to go deeper as followers of Christ.

Conflict 2 - Distraction

The next modern truth is that culture distracts us. We live in a technological world where we let our attention get directed by what is pretty, colorful, or appealing. This breeds distraction. Everyone expects everyone to be available all of the time. Our phone is always ringing, we put people on hold to take another call coming in, there are text messages coming in while our email is going off and someone is stopping by the house.

There is always something going on and we're always being distracted. When you are having a conversation with someone and your cell phone vibrates, you can't resist being curious whether it's a text, an email, or a picture. It's an illusion that fools us into feeling important when it actually robs us of our productivity.

Likewise, we think that we should be able to distract everyone else. So, whenever we get the urge, we just pick up the phone and call someone. Distraction and interruption steal more time than just about anything else today.

One of the things we need to do is learn to minimize and eliminate distractions and interruptions. We live in a culture where it's the norm versus the exception. We live in the culture of multi-tasking. We're doing a million things at once and I don't think we can change that. We're always going to have a lot to do, but we can direct how we do it.

As we progress or *regress* as a society, we are losing focus of what's most important. We are juggling too much. Our attention is getting fragmented and eventually the balls fall. What's worse, is that we can't even keep a few balls in the air long enough before we get distracted.

There are times during the day when you have to get certain tasks done, like getting the kids to school, paying the bills … eating, sleeping, working, studying, etc. You may have to "gather" your multi-tasking. We have to set aside a window of time so that it doesn't get out of control. It's having the mindset that we really have to minimize multi-tasking if we want to maximize productivity that counts the most.

When you enter a movie theater, your focus is enhanced. Outside distractions are cut off. The movie screen is large, and you are literally surrounded by sound. Similarly, your sense of accomplishment in this world will be enhanced if you put yourself physically, emotionally, and spiritually in a place where you can focus.

Conflict 3 - Instant Gratification

Another realization is that we are a culture of instant gratification, "we want it now", of "instant results". I think one of the underlying beliefs that hurts us the most is that there is legitimate snake oil that will solve our problems instantly. To some extent, the industrial revolution and technology advancements have made people weaker and more impatient.

The truth to this is staggering. We are developing technological advances that allow for us to cure things quickly in some cases, but the idea that there is a quick fix or a magic pill for the important things in life actually harms us. It's counter productive. For example, if you went to the dentist every time you had a toothache and his solution was a syringe of Novocain and a pair of pliers, before long you'd realize that a quick fix for one problem led to another.

Believing in instant results actually hurts us and that's what we've done with all aspects of life. The very idea of it is immaturity. It's the child in us. It's the ,"I want it now mommy" attitude and if we want to get results we have to grow past that. The goal here is to recognize it and avoid the culture of instant gratification. If we believe in it too much, it will only cause us to *regress* and create a mindset of impatience. Patience is one of the Fruits of the Spirit and we are called to act in accordance with it.

Conflict 4 - Choices

Another insight is that we live in a culture where we are overwhelmed by choices and those choices are confusing and steal time. One-hundred years ago, if you wanted to buy a car there weren't many options. Most people couldn't afford them anyway and so it was just a dream for most people. I've seen some of the first cars in a museum in Colorado Springs and there weren't many to choose from. Back then, we were limited to simple significant choices. Today, it's gotten to a point of overwhelm with the amount of, not only *significant* choices, but *insignificant ones* too.

If you want to buy a computer, where do you even start? There are so many different kinds of computers with so many different features. *"Do I buy the computer with the faster hard drive? Do I buy the computer with the bigger hard drive? Do I buy the faster processor or is it even going to make a difference? How much memory do I need? Which brand is best? Which one has the best customer service?"*

Investing time insignificantly can cause a heavy burden:

- People were born naked, now we spend absurd amounts of time on how we're going to decorate ourselves

- Bubble gum, chips, chicken noodle soup, soap, and dental floss all have over 20 varieties

It's too much choice that doesn't really make a difference. These insignificant choices are counterbalanced by the fact that most of us don't feel like we have enough personal choices, so this is a weird dichotomy. Here are some of the significant ones we struggle with focusing on:

- How we can impact the world for Jesus Christ

- Who we are

- What we can accomplish in a set period of time

The key here is learning the discipline of directing our attention. Understanding that not everything in our lives is of equal value even though it's placed in front of us. Even though others are caught in a pattern, God called us to use our time wisely and in different ways. Identifying where specifically we waste time and where we can redirect it is a starting point.

Conflict 5 - Entertainment

Another huge challenge that we face is that our culture is more concerned with entertainment vs. results, and we can see that on all levels.

When you watch a movie, you're more interested in being entertained by the movie than you are about the actual content or storyline. When you watch the news, you're more interested in who got murdered than you are in actual events taking place locally or abroad. When you eat a meal, you're more interested in how great it tastes than you are in fueling our body.

The culture of entertainment is stripping away all of the value underneath it. It just gives you the thin candy shell, or the thing that excites your emotions or senses. Entertainment is like a big cavity waiting to happen.

You have to realize that if you are going to grow and become healthy and productive, you can't be distracted with too much entertainment. You need to discipline yourself to focus on the things that get the most results.

In the long run, if you wind up entertaining yourself too much, you are going to entertain yourself to death. You're going to lose our ability to focus and you're not going to get the results you want. If you discipline yourself to only focus on what gets results, you'll learn to enjoy those things more and experience the long term benefit of it. When you grasp that fact, you will develop velocity in whatever area of your life you're pursuing moving forward.

Make the decision to move away from entertainment and do something that feeds your spirit, that feeds you on another level and helps you to develop into the person that you want to become. The more you do that, the more I think you'll find that it becomes a transforming experience, so beware of the culture of entertainment and avoid it as much as you possibly can.

Exercises

1. Identify the sources of disconnected information in each area of your life. Start with the areas in which you sense the most confusion.

2. What sources of wisdom will you seek-out to eliminate these problems …

3. Moving forward, how can you put in place a plan to evaluate which information and wisdom to incorporate into your life? (So you only work on what's significant and you don't get overwhelmed)

4. Identify where you have interruptions and distractions that … hinder you from being effective … stop you from finishing what you started … get in the way of being productive …

5. Identify where you multi-task the most.

6. Now, write down the things you can do to reduce or possibly eliminate the distractions and multi-tasking in your life.

7. Next, look inside your own life and pinpoint where you have an "immediate gratification" mentality.

8. How are you going to take concrete steps to change that?

9. Identify for yourself, where you have too many insignificant choices?

10. Now, identify where you don't have enough important choices?

11. Where and when are you over-exposed to entertainment?

12. What are better alternatives if you spent less time watching TV? Surfing the web? Being entertained?

This chapter may call for you to take some big steps, but they will be well worth it. Promise. So, take action on your answers and see how it effects your productivity.

Key objectives from this chapter

Recognition of society's conflicts with Christian values

Isolate the conflicts present in your life

Figure out how to keep them at bay

Chapter 7 – Completion

"Let us not become weary in doing good, for at the proper time we will reap a harvest if we do not give up. Therefore, as we have opportunity, let us do good to all people, especially to those who belong to the family of believers."

Galatians 6:9

Do you remember when you learned how to ride a two-wheeler? I remember the first stretch of sidewalk I conquered. How about your first loose tooth … was the best part when you pulled it out and looked in the mirror? Or how about when you had the exam for your drivers test. The best part was when it was over … right?

The challenge we encounter with these big leaps in life is that they're not always paved with a smooth path. When you were learning to ride that two-wheeler, didn't you fall? Take your first tooth, didn't it hurt? When you took the drivers test, wasn't there a ton of pressure on you to get it right? Pressure, pain, and struggle – the paths God gives us are all different and they all lead in two directions, either to give up or press forward when it hurts.

You might call this God's finishing process.

The Bible tells us about the process of sanctification, in which God is bringing us closer and closer to his image until the day we are lifted up from our worldly bodies into the heavens. Rather than give us a fish, he gave us a rod, reel, bait, and instructions to teach us how to catch the fish. He's given us the process, but not all of the outcomes. Throughout our lives, we develop our own completion.

Sometimes we put a ceiling between what we permit and forget that above that ceiling is what is possible with God. We have the ability to live within the freedom of God, not the confines of our own limitations. As we complete those things that are important, it moves us forward into the more detailed shape of our own unique freedom in Christ. From a child to an adult we have this finishing process happening with every decision we make.

As adults, there are lessons we can learn through the rocky roads in our lives, like:

- When we've been spread too thin

- When we haven't finished

- When we've been burdened

There's a funny thing that happens. We have ties to being comfortable and not interrupting how things are (even when they're going bad). The secret here is to untie ourselves *from ourselves* ... and *value moving forward over a lack of pain*. If we value a lack of pain more than progress, it will allow for us to be nearsighted and to just go with the flow of life, not realizing what's going on in the front end and what's coming out the back. If we value progress over the lack of pain, we will be able to be more conscious of the cycles that are present in our lives and to start directing the patterns.

Indecision

How about the *grey areas of life?* These are the biggest time wasters because we're considered to live in a culture that's post-modern now. Many people say "maybe" more than "yes" or "no" because they believe truth is relative and decisions follow suit. Indecision, hesitation, and non-confrontation can suck up life faster than a vacuum.

Certain things today just don't seem black and white, but they really are. We can be decisive and confident during life's most challenging obstacles. Business competitions, relationship struggles, family issues ... they can all be looked at with the same clarity.

Remember when original sin came into the world? Read Ezekiel 28:15-16 ... What was the cause?

The ground that spoiled the original bad fruit was motive ... Pride, Sin, Self-reliance. It's the same cause today. It's important to understand that there are some things people do, in God's eyes, that are clearly wrong:

- Busyness

- Idleness

- Gossip

However, it's harder to identify an action that is clearly right. Giving your time can be right if your intent is right, but if your intent is wrong the action is also wrong. The same goes with giving your resources.

What makes a decision a good decision is your motive. The good motives you have behind trying to manage your time and pave these new paths. Good motives to free yourself from unnecessary indecision, that's what's important to God and <u>it is</u> black and white!

Procrastination

As Chicago grew from a cow town to a metropolis, streets and buildings were raised up out of the mud. The streets were wide and unnamed, carved by cow paths, not city planners. The curves are organic and confusing to someone not familiar with the area. Once it was industrialized, the city planners decided to go with the flow. The paths of least resistance were chosen for the design. Today, the process is known for it's historical symbolism, but definitely not for the progress it allows. They made a quick and significant decision.

Can we make great decisions quickly?

Do we all believe that to make progress you need to take your time, carefully create and consider all the options and then make a final choice? Or is that just an excuse for procrastination and avoidance? This is what many people consider the ideal decision-making process. Yet, in the real world we know:

- Time is short

- Perfect information is not available

- You do not know the full impact of your choices

Realistically, we can't draw out decisions in order to have a comfortable transition. This is one of the basic elements of procrastination. Joseph Ferrari, Ph.D., associate professor of psychology at De Paul University in Chicago, and Timothy Pychyl, Ph.D., associate professor of psychology at Carleton University in Ottawa, Canada have identified some characteristics of procrastination:

- 20% of people are chronic procrastinators

- Procrastinators look for distractions

- Procrastination causes health and behavioral problems

They identify that there are three types of procrastinators:

- The last minute thrill-seeker

- The fear-of-success (or failure) avoider

- The non-responsible indecisive

Spending more and more time on a decision is not always a smart and effective thing. Most people think it is, but then they never get anything done. In order to make important decisions quickly, you need guidance. Here's where an intent on completion and practice making decisions is important. So, what does the Bible say about this? Read the following scriptures.

- Luke 12:40
- Matthew 5:23-25 and 37
- Luke 14:16- 21

The truth is that procrastination is ineffectiveness in it's habitual form. God doesn't want it for us and neither do we.

Exercises

You're going to do an exercise that will help you get some completion and finish up anything that's piled up over time.

If there is a 1:1 ratio between the depth and breadth of your belief and the rightness and goodness of what you get done, there will be no way to stop you. The reason that things fail to get done is due to a lack of belief. Jesus called us to commitment. As a matter of fact, people who go about issues without commitment, tend to lead very hollow lives. Their belief is lacking, that's why it's so important. The critical element to doing good and carrying out tasks that have overwhelmed you in the past is whether you care or not. It's important to life as well and central to our character.

- What would happen if you had the ability to gain completion in the areas that really mean the most to you in life?

On the other hand, sometimes we care so much, that we spread ourselves as thin as possible in order to please those around us and inadvertently overwhelm ourselves in the process.

- What would happen if you no longer allowed others to abuse your time, generosity or expertise?

In my studies of the Bible (and through several different first hand situations) I've learned that unfinished tasks, carrying burdens, and the open doors in our lives make us weary. They draw from our resources. Something that is incomplete, maybe an unresolved argument you had with someone a year ago, maybe an unfinished project. You need to get some closure and completion in those areas of your life where there is none.

The first part of the exercise is to:

- Make a list of all the areas in your life where you don't have completion.

And by the way, I'll key you in here, when we have incompletion we usually have denial.

Make a list of each area of your life, each issue that is lacking completion, when you're done, come back and read the rest of this section. GO …

Hopefully it was a little eye-opening to look at that list of things that you have incomplete in your life. Some of the things might be chores, some of them might be relationships or even obligations that have been forgotten.

Next :

- Go through the list and prioritize them by number. The ones that are making you weary just thinking about them, those are the ones that we want to attack first.
- Find the 20% that are sucking the 80% of your strength and either complete them or let them go.

Here's an example: If your roof is leaking … fix it. If you bought something, it broke, and you lost the receipt so the store won't take it back, either choose to let it go or state your case for a replacement. Press through until you are happy with the result because it's not worth the energy that you are giving it under the surface by letting it stay unfinished.

This might take some mercy versus justice, but the point is that you need to get completion whatever that means. It might mean talking to someone that you haven't talked to in 3 years and telling them you're sorry or that you forgive them. Just get closure! Tie it up, put a bow on it once and for all and don't let it hang out there anymore.

We're going to finish this section right now and you should prioritize and then go get completion on the top 20%. Just do what it takes, either get some completion or release it. That's going to be a process that frees up a tremendous amount of your time and spirit. So do that right now.

Key objectives from this chapter

Understood procrastination

Uncovered incomplete important items

Completion!

Chapter 8 – Focus

"he is a double-minded man, unstable in all he does."
James 1:8

Improving your external life, i.e. – career, ministry, finance, or relationships - starts with what you believe about yourself … *internally*. When you changed your beliefs about who Jesus Christ was to you, *internally*, your perception changed externally. If you *believe* that you can make more progress in life, then you understand the will of God. His intent for you to be fruitful and multiply serves to propel your actions in getting things done. The key is … you really have to believe without any division of spirit.

Remember from the beginning … 1 Corinthians 2:16 says:

"… we have the mind of Christ"

Read Matthew 6:24. Belief is an interesting thing because it is intangible. You can't see it on someone and we can't always immediately recognize the lack of it inside ourselves. When we start to allow double-mindedness or other priorities to creep in and short circuit our thinking … we have to be really aware in order to cut to the source.

If our wires get crossed it hinders our progress. We start to think less of ourselves and the things we can accomplish in life. We settle for less than we should. The source of that *stinking thinking* is the lie of sin. If we allow that intrusion into our lives, accept what it tells us regarding what we can or cannot accomplish, it lessens our effectiveness. Here's an example:

- If you ask a child to sing a song, most will belt one out quicker then you can finish the request
- If you ask an adult, most will say they can't sing because they weren't made to

Now, read Matthew 18:3.

Look back to some of the answers you've uncovered and ask yourself:

- How many other people in the world are already doing what God desires me to do in my life?

For instance:

- Do you believe God can really bring you to the point of productivity you are striving for?
- Is it true that the important aspects of your life can increase and you can still be a faithful servant of Christ?
- Are there ways to impact the world for Jesus from where you are right now?

Do you really … really … believe these statements?

When we see that someone else has already done, learned, or became, something in life, why is it our first reaction to shy back and question God's ability to do the same in us? Too often we allow spiritual and mental limitations to get in the way of our God-given potential, but God's power is limitless. We get defeated or confused and we start to believe negative thoughts internally and then we carry out those thoughts externally.

Scripture gives an example of what happens when we give our minds over to this captive thinking. Read 2 Timothy 3:2 as an extreme example and you can see where a mixed perspective of truth and lies ultimately leads. We have to surrender to truth in every area of our lives. Compare the verse in Timothy to 2 Corinthians 10:5. Think about it.

Calculate the value of each decision everyday

When you are faced with a decision to seek truth, righteous, and productivity, or something else like avoidance or comfort, which do you typically choose? How do those small choices add up to eternal significance?

Some decisions have automatic after affects. God has designed us with many little mechanisms within our bodies and beliefs are no different. Think about how the decision to eat a piece of food has an automatic effect … the way your digestive system breaks it down … sends nutrients in the right direction … and affects your overall health … or how the decision of your mood affects the way you relate to others.

Your beliefs come in small little packages that add up to your encompassing belief system that runs the operations for who you are. You have a packaged belief of who you are as a child … parent … student … mother … Christian … worker … friend … athlete … competitor … leader … servant … soldier … teacher … speaker … the way you see yourself physically … the way you communicate … your manners … the pressure you can handle … what you can accomplish … the amount of sleep you need … every aspect of your life.

In order to eternally succeed we need to align our thinking with God-centered ideals versus worldly ideas. The truth is that these beliefs of ourselves are ever-changing and not based in *who we were.* They are based on *who we are becoming in Christ.* We should base our self-image in the future and measure it by our rebirth in Jesus Christ. God has called us to adapt to his likeness each moment and leave the limiting lies behind. Our lives and actions should be of continual increase.

Sometimes when the baseline of our belief is divided we get to a point where we can no longer evaluate where we stand and how to take action. It's a limitation of our beliefs and there's a direct relationship with the unity of our belief and the unity of our actions. A simple way of thinking about it is *"The More You Believe, The More You Achieve."*

When double mindedness creeps in, you can't be fully effective with anything you're involved in.

The tragedy is that even though you may have good intent in making forward progress, if you're pulling from two different sources, if you're beliefs aren't formatted properly with God fully guiding you, searching scripture and seeking wise counsel, you are probably running at 50% of the efficiency that you could be.

Exercises

1. Now you're going to make a list of anything you do where *you feel* double-minded. Walk *yourself* from a typical Monday morning to a typical Sunday evening and visualize your routines to pinpoint where *you* lack focus in your life.

Examples

• At dinner ... thinking about priorities elsewhere

• Leading meetings ... mind on next task

• In traffic ... mind wandering through day

2. Where *others* perceive me of being distracted or disengaged? This is a *perspective* exercise so you're going to do your best to *step outside of yourself* and look from the eyes of those who are important to you. This is a difficult and challenging task so take your time. The point of this is not to seek the approval of others (we seek the approval of Christ), but to look at yourself from another perspective.

More Examples

• Tell people one thing – Really believe or feel another

• Worshiping at church – Pre-occupied with other thoughts

• On the job – Mentally detached

Question # 3 is going to be the culmination of the first two questions. The tie-in of this chapter is about becoming aware of what's really important in your life. What are the things you are trying to do that you could be doing better? How can you focus more time on those things?

Go back and look at your list of double-minded and distraction areas and find the one area out of the two you need to focus on to really see the important God-centered results in your life. You will do that by answering the following question …

3. Where should you really be investing your attention? What is going to lead to eternal significance in the eyes of Jesus Christ?

Next, I'm sure you've found that doing these types of exercises is enlightening, but also a little bit challenging because you realize "Wow, new perspective. I can focus!" So, circle those things you need to focus on and just do it. Go for them and prepare yourself to dig into the final chapter.

Key objectives from this chapter

Understand the link between belief and action

Build solid belief bridges

Recognize double-mindedness

Chapter 9 – Transformation

"Do not conform any longer to the pattern of this world, but be transformed by the renewing of your mind. Then you will be able to test and approve what God's will is—his good, pleasing and perfect will."
Romans 12:2

There's something really compelling about our perception. The funny thing is, who we think we are is completely subjective. It's based on what we take in and not at all who we truly are. The whole concept of perception and identity isn't something you can label anyway. Our identity is always changing and the Bible tells us it's constantly moving forward in the image of God (even during struggles as we saw in the last chapter).

Take a look at how we perceive ourselves and the world around us. Imagine your view of others who are different than you. The Bible shows us many instances of perception and how it can change. How we allow our own perception to change will be a foundation for the progress we make in life.

For example:

- Picture yourself in your mind right now

- Now ask your 3 closest friends to tell you who they think you are

- Then ask your 3 closest relatives …

>   *The truth is … those 3 pictures will be different*

Perception is unique and individual. Look back at your past and see how much of yourself you recognize today? We can't avoid the fact that our outside is sometimes shaped by cultural particulars. It happens. But, we can be secure and dig deeper into the truth of who we are as ever transforming and changing children of God.

The need to face the truth about our change in relation to God, our relationships with one another, and the results of our actions is a consistent biblical theme:

Let's look at Genesis 32:22-31 together

- Jacob wrestles with a shadowy adversary

- Jacob is then named Israel

- This is about his need to face the truth of who he is so that God can transform him

In 1 Corinthians 13:12 it's looking ahead to the time when our knowledge of ourselves in relation to God is as clear as God's knowledge of us. Romans 12:3 calls us to think realistically of ourselves from the perspective of what God thinks is important. Much of Jesus' life was about inviting people to face the truth about themselves:

- Mark 10:17-23: the rich young man
- Luke 7: 36-50: Jesus' dinner with Simon the Pharisee
- The letters to the churches in Revelation

I've always put pen to paper in regards to what I wanted to "become", perception wise, in my life. Here's a sampling of what I mean from when I was in the Army …
- Have highest team Physical Fitness scores
- Become Non-Commissioned Officer of the year
- Finish #1 in Brigade ruck march …

Here's a couple years later …
- Run a marathon
- Become employee of the year
- Purchase our dream home …

I've since analyzed what my goals were all focused on, and I've discovered some insights that have helped me and can help you.

I was doing my best to maximize _my_ potential …

…not the potential of Christ in me. Trying to chase after your own potential is a losing battle, because it doesn't exist. You may accomplish many things in life, but ultimately they will take you more into yourself and less into Christ. In short, I was setting myself up to feel like an egomaniac or a narcissist until I aligned my identity in Christ with my actions.

When God really started to lay his hand on me, the flavor of my goals changed completely. They're now my **Goals for Christ**…
- I will be focused on the time I am given in my life to best serve God's purposes

- I will develop an evangelical spiritual growth plan for myself and those around me
- I will set an unyielding example of excellence to my family in Christ

I've gone from random notes in my wallet to laminated pages detailing the potential of Christ in me. These pages provide me with a concrete picture of what I sense to be God's will in my life. They spell out and paint the picture of who I am striving to be in the identity He's given me today.

I have these on my wall now. They act as a target. They keep me focused on my goals and the important areas of my life. I'll let you in on a secret though, as I really got in touch with who Jesus Christ was calling me to become, <u>I was forced to take massive action.</u> You might be too!

Life will direct people as long as people let life direct them, but when we finally come to the revelation that our identity is not in line with who we've become … that we've lost perspective … it causes massive action because we've been confronted with the truth.

Habits

So far, we've canvassed ourselves and painted the picture we call *us*. But what makes *us*… well…*us?* They're the things we call habits. Habits are the automatic responses that have been so embedded into ourselves that we no longer take the time to think or feel. We just act. The things we do, the places we go, the stuff that fills our days.

Changing habits is difficult

Understanding this and preparing for it will give you a leg up on overcoming the process that occurs. Read 2 Corinthians 10:5. Regardless of the habit, whether it's dropping a bad one, acquiring a new one, or becoming better in life, the way habit change occurs is always the same because the process is about overcoming. Titus 2:11-12 sums it up.

Additionally, there are three main obstacles you have to fight against in order for bad habits to stop:

1. The World

2. The Enemy

3. The Flesh

The cultural conflicts of this world are a big part of overcoming habits. The world systems are used to invigorate sin and complacency. Once we come to the recognition and realization of these forces, we are able to boldly confront them and work against their unfruitful patterns. Read James 4:4.

Our new Christian life begins with salvation and continues on with the transformation of our thoughts and actions. As followers of Christ we are set apart. The hard part is, Jesus never called us to act differently in private, he told us to be different *amongst the lost.*

This truth requires personal habit transformation along with another even more difficult task … *public integration.*

Surveys have shown that the fear of death is only trumped by the fear of speaking in public. Jesus didn't call us to retreat and separate. He called us to persuade righteousness and the good news upon the lost, but we do this from the inside out and the only way to do this is to be among the lost. When we progress in the areas God has called us to … it's a testimony to others.

So, tying All of these biblical truths, concepts, exercises and what you've discovered about yourself really begins to mean something important …

True perception really means having heard the Gospel and belief in Jesus.

Changing habits really means becoming Christ-like.

Transformation means being obedient to God's perfect will in your life.

From here I'd like to give you some of the more important personal insights that have helped me in my life.

7 Insights

Before God revealed my calling to ministry, I used to travel quite a bit. I've been blessed to be able to dig into the particulars of several industries including finance, technology, agriculture and defense based on the experience. Along with God's will, having this type of familiarity allows you to see patterns. You can walk away with a deeper understanding of what behaviors cause a person to be successful and those that cause a person to fail in what they are striving for.

For instance, at a financial services conference, you'll see a guy who's been in the business 20 years scraping the lunch tray between sessions and beside him, a 35 year old guy wearing a pin that shows he's managing millions of dollars. You figure, one of them is doing really well and the other is maybe a bit displaced in his calling.

For most in that industry, finance equates to success, stewardship and reward. In it, there are bottom line results. Funny thing is, you will see the same patterns across all industries. But the gap, the difference, and the result doesn't come from the performance, it comes from belief!

You see, everyone believes in something. Where we place that belief however, is what makes all the difference. If our belief in what we undertake is weak then our results will be lacking. It's a divide that can be bridged ... if you know how. And I want to help you avoid some of the traps that I've identified that stop people from living out their purposes in life.

Insight 1 – Work for Jesus Christ (Colossians 3:23-24)

We had just sat down for lunch at another conference. One of the attendees there started to talk about his faith. I asked him, "How does your faith relate to your business?"

He hesitated. He explained that his business was a completely separate thing. Well, that's not right. It's all about Jesus Christ. If you're doing something that isn't focused on Christ, stop doing it.

It's okay to admit we sometimes overlook these walls. Time and again people do it, but God and our lives tell otherwise. That's a problem. It equates Jesus as just another "part" of life.

Better to admit you are doing it now than to try to hide it. What message is that sending to those around you? It's sending a message that it's okay and excusable to continue on like that, and if your goal is to focus on eternity, the good news is there's a better way.

When you make it acceptable to live in a way that doesn't honor Jesus, that's when the problems occur. You're justifying behavior that is counter productive to God's will for you … to bear fruit!

Jesus said "I am the truth" and I agree.

It's only when you look at your situation with truth, that you can formulate a plan based in reality and on eternity. Otherwise, you'll come up with excuses.

People are either really good at honoring Jesus or really good at making excuses, but no one's good at both.

There's another easy choice!

Insight 2 – Regroup to Move Forward (Acts Chapter 1)

The apostles regrouped after Judas defected. They had to discern God's will in order to make progress.

I used to be way too thorough. Writing almost as much as I heard. Once I attended an event where I almost caught my pen on fire writing so fast. Know how many of those notes I referred back to? About 5%. Ask my wife.

The fact is, I know exactly where God's taking me. I may not know how, but I'm only interested in the wisdom and ideas that will get me there much faster or enhance what I'm already doing. If it's not moving me more toward Christ, it's not for me.

Some people that leave church or events leave with pages and pages of notes. I used to be one of them. Let's be honest with ourselves. Are we doing anything with the notes when we get home? Is it adding to the clutter? Are we taking action?

There is a point when you need to regroup. When you have too much noise that's usually caused by trying to take in 24 hours of ideas in 2 hours over and over. 2 condensed hours covering thousands of hours of experience. There's too much knowledge on the table without enough action.

When you leave yourself open to everything, you end up choosing nothing.

Here's what you need to do ... always be working on one thing.

That's not attractive to most people though. In fact, it kind of sounds like hard work, doesn't it? That's because it is... in a relative sense. You're going to have to dig in for a bit.

Here's how you beat clutter. First, *realize it exists.* Second, whenever you feel it, *stop thinking.* Clutter only comes from thinking too much. What do you do instead of over-thinking something? *Take action.* Anything is better than staying in a state of overwhelm.

Insight 3 - Choose (2 Samuel 24:12, 1 Chronicles 21:11-13)

Here's a rule of thumb. Choices in life can be hard, but waiting until the last minute is even harder. Take no longer than 60 seconds to make a choice. Here's the simplest one question formula for any decision you will ever make in your life:

1. What are my options?

Then, figure out which option is best and decide! Delaying the decision is worse than making the wrong decision. You can usually fix bad decisions. You can't fix indecision.

Insight 4 - "Harder" is "Easier" (Genesis Chapter 1 with emphasis on verse 27)

When you take the road less traveled, you lean on the creative power of God … and that's good. It's an interesting fact that if something is "just a little bit harder" for most people to create, it makes God's creativity in you stand out more.

Don't think easier... think harder.

Look for those things that require just a little more effort. Those are the things you want to do, because most people won't do them. If you do that enough, you'll start to develop advantages in life and for Christ.

Insight 5 - The Importance of Community (Acts 4:32)

Being a Christian means that information is not as important as people. Sometimes we get caught up trying to know-it-all, but that's just something we do for our sense of security. You wouldn't believe how many people don't focus on information, but have a lot of faith and a lot of fellowship and God protects them from what they may not have encountered yet in life.

Why? It's God's will in their life. Period. They have the right counsel. People who help and care for them. People who have endorsed the Holy Spirit in them. People who have put them in contact with the right opportunities and resources.

People are much more important than information.

Having four close friends will probably help you more than reading four Christian novels this month. We all have access to good information, but good people are hard to find. Don't fool yourself, if you are. Spend more time making friends and introducing people to Christ. The best way to do that is just like Jesus did, expecting nothing in return. If you do that with enough people, you'll be well on your way.

Insight 6 - Be Blessed (Deuteronomy 28:1-14)

Don't underestimate the unseen. I believe it's the difference in most of our endeavors.

God has done and will continue to do miraculous things in our lives.

Expect them.

Someone once said "the harder I work, the luckier I get". I believe it's the more "blessed we get." What's the takeaway? It means that if you're currently doing a lot of things right, but aren't getting huge life results right away, don't get discouraged. If you stay at it long enough, you'll eventually see God working in your life. Sometimes sooner than later.

Being blessed has a lot to do with it. God's path for you is another.

Insight 7 – Rest in Faith (Matthew 11:29-30, Hebrews 1:1-11)

Here's my life: Leverage my gifts and talents to multiply God's word. Focus on outreach and bringing people to Christ. Acknowledge God in everything I do. Repeat the process.

That's it. Simple. I could write it on a post-it note.

I really only do 4 or 5 things well my life.

I am good at them. I'm not an expert at a lot of things, but I am great at keeping things simple. I'm thoughtful in creating value for others. I'm creative in introducing change in my life and that of those around me, and I'm great at managing my time to get the most done.

Wow, that's not a lot, is it? But, it's all I really need. Really, just master a few simple elements and put them together in your life. We have a propensity as people to try to learn everything about everything and complicate life. If we put too much noise in our heads, we never get things done.

You need to clear the noise. Be able to write your goals on a post it note... If you can't do that, you need to simplify even more.

Exercises

1.   What areas of your perception are you trying to improve and how can you address them now?

Here's a tip. These are usually the things we hold on to that will make the biggest difference if we challenge them to change.

2. What do you picture when you imagine being more *"tuned-in"* to your identity in Christ from this point forward?

3. What is the most important measure of your identity aside from finances , material possessions, or friendships?

4. How does your identity affect your progress in life?

5. What do you do when you really feel good about yourself? How can you transfer this enthusiasm to others to influence them to do good?

6. If you wrote some **Goals for Christ**, what would they say?

7. What habits are you going to change in order to get more God in your life?

8. Is there anything you might lose as a result of doing this? Is it worth it?

9. What would happen if you could change habits in all these areas?

10. What is the most significant personal insight you have received from this entire process?

Key objectives from this chapter

Understand perception

Change habits

Get forward insight

Notes

Index

Action..38, 56

Advantage...46

Balance...26

Benefits...29

Challenges...67

Choices...68, 75, 106

Clarity...16

Comfort...20

Completion...81, 88, 98

Conflicts..71

Corinthians..................7, 40, 90, 92, 97, 99, 125, 126

Distraction..72, 73

Enemy..38, 39, 100

Entertainment...76

Exercises.............9, 21, 35, 55, 68, 77, 86, 93, 109

Fear..18, 19

Focus...90, 108

Freedom...17, 19, 31, 32

God 1, 2, 5, 6, 8, 11, 12, 13, 17, 18, 19, 20, 21, 23, 24, 26, 27, 28, 29, 30, 31, 32, 33, 34, 35, 36, 42, 43, 44, 45, 46, 47, 48, 50, 51, 52, 53, 54, 55, 59, 60, 61, 62, 63, 64, 65, 66, 67, 69, 71, 76, 81, 82, 83, 84, 86, 90, 91, 92, 93, 95, 96, 97, 98, 99, 100, 102, 103, 104, 105, 106, 107, 108, 110, 123

Habits...99

Identity...59

Indecision...83

Information..1, 2, 71

Insight...104, 105, 106, 107, 108

Isaiah..55, 125

Jesus 2, 3, 4, 5, 8, 9, 11, 17, 18, 19, 20, 21, 26, 29, 30, 31, 32, 33, 34, 38, 40,
    41, 42, 43, 45, 46, 47, 48, 50, 52, 53, 54, 58, 60, 62, 63, 64, 65, 66, 67,
    76, 86, 90, 91, 93, 95, 97, 99, 100, 102, 104, 105, 107, 123

John...26, 32, 60, 63, 66, 123, 125

Luke...62, 85, 97, 125, 126

Mark...97, 126

Matthew.....................4, 5, 7, 8, 34, 38, 42, 60, 64, 85, 90, 91, 108, 125, 126

Money...38, 40

Organization...1

Persecution..38, 39

Prayer...23, 51

Priorities...44, 46, 48, 51, 52, 54

Procrastination...84, 85

Reduction...58

Romans..3, 18, 28, 32, 48, 96, 97, 125, 126

To-Do list...23

Transformation...48, 96

Worry...38, 40

Credits & Thanks

No book would be complete without credit where credit is due. *Ex nihilo* is a Latin phrase that means *"out of nothing"*. This is how God created us. From that point on, everything is a product of biblical truth and collective wisdom. In the creation of this book I'd like to thank the following people and organizations for the contributions of their wisdom, insights, and/or directly making this book possible:

Jesus Christ

My entire extended family

A.W. Tozer

Alan Stringfellow

blueletterbible.org

Brian Tracy

createspace.com

Dan Sullivan

David Villarreal

Dr. Joseph Ferrari

Dr. Robert Cialdini

Dr. Timothy Pychyl

Greg Asimakoupoulos

Heartland Christian School

James Dobson

Jeff Slosson

John MacArthur

John Maxwell

Kevin Fleming

Larry Osborne

Logos Software

Ray Edwards

Refuge Bible Church

Ron Jackson

Rich Riche

Sally Stuart

Steve McKinley

The Johnson family

The U.S. Army

Willy & Sarah Jane Roberts

William Strunk, Jr.

… and everyone reading

Scripture References

Chapter 1

Psalm 119:133, Romans 6:23, Matthew 8:18-22, Matthew 6:5, Hebrews 8:5, Matthew 6:6, 1 Corinthians 2:16, Matthew 17:20, Psalm 5:12, Genesis 6-8

Chapter 2

Deuteronomy 4:20, Hebrews 3-16,18-19, Romans 1:1, Philippians 6:11, 2 Timothy 2:16

Chapter 3

Psalms 89:47, Acts 2:42-47, Genesis 1:1, Joshua 10:13-14, Ecclesiastes 3:1-8, Romans 12:2, Hosea 10:12, Genesis 1:27, Ecclesiastes 7:29, John 8:31-32, Romans 8:14, 2 Timothy 4:1-2, 2 Peter 1:5-8, Matthew 6, Proverbs 4:18, Psalms 49:5,

Chapter 4

James 1:22, Matthew 13:3-9 & 18-23, Ephesians 2:6, 2 Timothy 3:12, Philippians 4:12, Hebrews 11:1, 2 Corinthians 1:3-4, Acts 5, Matthew 8:18-27, Proverbs 27:1, James 4:13-15, Proverbs 6:6, 13:4, 20:4, 26:15, Galatians 5:22-26, Genesis 2:7, Acts 17:18, Proverbs 3, Romans 12:1-2, 1 Peter 4:7, Ephesians 5:15-16, Acts 6:2-4, Isaiah 43:18-19

Chapter 5

2 Timothy 2:20, Matthew 16:13, John 18:33-38, John 14:6, John 1:12, 15:16, Colossians 2:9-10, Philippians 3:20, 1 Peter 2:9, Acts 2:14-47, Luke 15:3-7, Acts 17:22-34, Matthew 12:34-37, James 2:8, 2 Timothy 4:10, John 6:1-21, Ezekiel 16:49

Chapter 6

Hosea 4:6

Chapter 7

Galatians 6:9, Ezekiel 28:15-16, Luke 12:40, Matthew 5:23-25 & 37, Luke 14:16-21

Chapter 8

James 1:8, 1 Corinthians 2:16, Matthew 6:24, Matthew 18:3, 2 Timothy 3:2, 2 Corinthians 10:5

Chapter 9

Romans 12:2, Genesis 32:22-31, 1 Corinthians 13:12, Romans 12:3, Mark 10:17-23, Luke 7:36-50, 2 Corinthians 10:5, Titus 2:11-12, Colossians 3:23-24, Acts 1, 2 Samuel 24:12, 1 Chronicles 21:11-13, Genesis 1:27, Acts 4:32, Deuteronomy 28:1-14, Matthew 11:29-30, Hebrews 1:1-11

Do You Believe In Jesus?

This book may make it into the hands of someone who does not yet know Jesus Christ as their savior. That person may just be you. No matter how you feel right now, it's possible. It is for that reason alone that I must offer the time to confront this challenging and sobering question.

Why should I "Believe in Jesus"?

We are all sinners, lawbreakers, born corrupted and are under the condemnation of God's Law. The Bible says that God is holy and without flaw and we are not. Regardless of how you feel about who you are, by birth, stature, or significance, without Jesus Christ, your permanent, eternal residence is by default, Hell. Regardless of you accepting this or not, it's true. Placing yourself in a state of denial doesn't stop the seconds from ticking on the clock and the truth that without believing in Jesus Christ you are now awakened and conscious of this fact.

The truth is, there is not a single man-made philosophy that has a cure for this state. There is no "religion" or proposition that can answer all of the deepest probing questions of our minds, desires, and hearts to cure the problem of sin. Right now sin has mastery over your life and that mastery will continue to increase until you find the cure.

But it wasn't always that way and it's not God's desire for you . . .

139

Acknowledge Your Sin

First, open your eyes. Sin is tragic, disgusting, vile, pornographic, abusive, chaotic … it destroys and leads to spiritual death. It has eternal results . . . the stark separation from God and everything good.

Not everyone is willing to acknowledge their sin. Some people are not able to see this truth. It requires complete honesty.

Repent

Repent and turn to God, so that your sins may be completely forgiven and forgotten. Repentance is a complete inward change that results in a progressive outward change. You must change your heart toward sin and want God to end it's mastery over you. After all, sin is such a horrible disease it took God sending his son, Jesus Christ, to die and make forgiveness possible for you.

Most people are afraid to be vulnerable and hand this over to God. They feel once something is done, it's done. The truth is, sin leaves marks and it's your choice to erase them.

Believe in Jesus Christ

"For God so loved the world that he gave His only begotten Son, that whoever believes in Him shall not perish but have eternal life" – John 3:16. You must believe that Christ substituted Himself for you, that He died for your sins, and that He was resurrected from death. Jesus conquered sin and death so that he could redeem you as God's child.

The world today is a place where people believe that the highest form of life is themselves. That just isn't true. There is a righteous God with a perfect law and an plan of redemption from sin. *Will you accept it?*

Make Your Decision

If you confess with your mouth, "Jesus is Lord" and believe in your heart that God raised Him from the dead, you will be saved. It's so hard, it's easy. You must believe in Christ and receive Him personally into your life by faith to be saved from the power of sin and the eternity of Hell.

Will you believe and pray -

> "God, I know I am a sinner, and that Christ alone can save me. I repent of my sin and believe Jesus Christ died for me. I want to receive Him as my personal Savior."

If you have now accepted Jesus Christ as your personal savior, please let me know about your decision. Find a Bible believing church to disciple you and start being a strong witness for Jesus Christ.

Joe Luna

For more information about Joe's ministry, to become a part of our newsletter, or to share how God has used this book in your life, feel free to write:

Joe Luna

P.O. Box 413

Council Bluffs, IA 51502-413

or visit us at:

www.joelunablog.com

Made in the USA
Charleston, SC
18 June 2010